About Blossom Goodchild

Blossom was born in England. She fulfilled her childhood dream to become an actress and has toured extensively in repertoire and musicals throughout the U.K.

In December 2000 she moved to Australia and now resides in Noosa Heads, Queensland with her husband Goody and son Ritchie where she continues her acting career along with her spiritual work.

Walking in the Light and the Love

The Wisdom of 'White Cloud'
Channelled by
Blossom Goodchild

A percentage of the proceeds from the sale of this book will be donated to "Dolphin Aid Australia".

Published by
Joshua Books
P.O.Box 5149, Maroochydore BC
Queensland Australia 4558

For enquiries concerning "Walking in the Light and the Love" and for information on Blossom Goodchild / White Cloud, e-mail to "richalstead@austarnet.com.au"

Editors note: We have endeavoured to keep as much of "White Cloud's" grammar, turns of phrase and terminology as possible – in a few cases we have altered the grammar to make the sense of the message easier to understand and to clarify some points. - Ric Halstead

Copyright © 2003 Blossom Goodchild

All rights reserved. No part of this publication may be reproduced, stored in a retrieval system, or transmitted, in any form or by any means without the prior written permission of the publisher, nor be otherwise circulated in any form of binding or cover other than that in which it is published and without a similar condition being imposed on the subsequent purchaser.

ISBN 0 9751594 0 2

Category : New Age: Channelled Writings : Author

www.joshuabooks.com

DEDICATION

I dedicate this book to the energy known as White Cloud and all 'unseen' friends throughout our universes who strive to assist those who have chosen to live on this Earth plane at this exciting time.

Golden Rays!

Blossom

(August 2003)

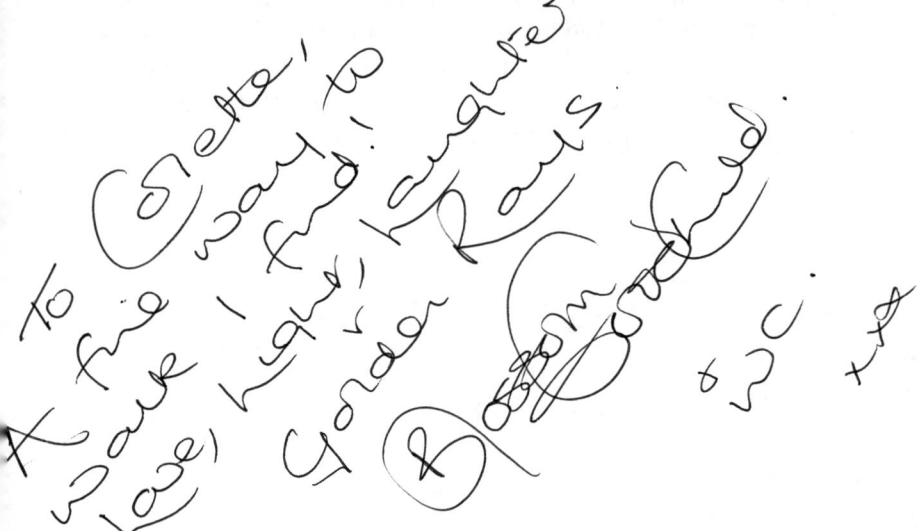

ACKNOWLEDGEMENTS

Of course I must begin with White Cloud for suggesting and providing the material for the book!
For his wisdom, compassion, humour and devotion - for the laughter we share - for the exhilaration working together brings - but most of all - above all - I thank him for his unconditional Love.

Golden Rays to you my friend and Thank you. ..

Always at your service.

IN ENGLAND

Thank you to Heather, wherever you maybe now, for showing me how to link up with White Cloud and for your Love.
Thank you to Deb and Ian for their encouragement and assistance.
Thank you to Angela for her friendship and devotion to the cause.
Special thanks to Alex for the most awesome painting on the cover. An avid fan of White Cloud, and he of her. I guess that's why he asked her to do the painting. Thank you also for your 100% attendance at the meetings and for being the most beautiful example of a human being! Her stunning artwork can be viewed on www.alexmarler.co.uk.

IN OZ

Thank you to all whom attend the various meetings.
A special thank you to the Monday group.
These are: Goody, Jill, Luke, Jennah, Lizzie, Jeanette, Eileen, Ric, Nita and Kerri. What can I say guys? As White Cloud says 'If you were not there to listen, there would be no tapes to

transcribe, and we would look pretty stupid sitting there talking to no-one'.
To each one of you I thank you for your friendship, support and loyalty.

Special thanks to:

Ric for the final editing and so willingly and enthusiastically taking care of all technicalities involved regarding publishing. Just could not have done it without you. Heaven sent!

Eileen for the thought and time put into the Forward and for her laughter, friendship, lightheartedness and for sharing my days.

Naomi of "Energy to you" for her spiritual insight in designing the cover.

Ritchie, my son, for staying in his bedroom during the meetings and not making a sound and for generally accepting a Native American into the family!

Special, special thanks to my husband Goody! - for his patience and understanding - for his easy acceptance of watching his wife turn into a chappy in public and most of all for his trust and Love. Words in this case are inadequate!

So many souls have entered my life due to White Cloud. Some stay, some just pass through. I would like to thank all those who took the time to participate in a meeting or personal reading. Each session allows us to experience another connection and through this, our working together has turned into quite a little double act!

THANK YOU ALL

Blossom

FOREWARD

If you have chosen this book, or it is in your possession, trust that it is meant to be there. Trusting and knowing that 'all is as should be' is one of White Cloud's most prominent themes.

I was introduced to White Cloud whilst studying my Masters in the field of Neuro Linguistic Programming. As in all things, I believe this was pre-destined for when the pupil is ready, the teacher will come.

Along with other great teachers or mentors, White Cloud relies on metaphors and symbols to get his message across so the individual recipient can take from it whatever is appropriate to their own needs. His usual method is to show Blossom pictures and images and she then relays them out loud. His choice of symbols is never by chance. The images are so simple that it is easy to visualise them and often you can comprehend immediately what message he is trying to convey. If however you were to ponder deeply upon these symbolisms, there is often a far greater meaning behind them all.

Often White Cloud will present the same message expressed in a variety of ways. In his gentle way, he reminds us that it can be useful to look at things from a different perspective. A common thread among the stories is that life is all about love.

I feel honoured to be a member of the group that meets with White Cloud regularly where I have received so much solace, wisdom, understanding and acceptance. He has inspired me to put love into everything and thus my life has reached different heights from what it was.

My role here is to try to 'create the scene' as authentically as I can, so that you, the reader, can gain the greatest benefit from his words of wisdom. Whether it is an individual or a group reading, the feeling that permeates is one of awe, excitement and trust that we will be experiencing unconditional love. White Cloud makes each person feel so special by giving them a story about the Light that they are. There is a comfort in knowing that he is sharing his knowledge to be of assistance to others and that the intention behind any of his messages is to contribute to the good of all. It is also a lesson in faith - knowing that everything, during a reading and indeed in life, has a reason.

Like the messages chosen, the words spoken are not used by accident. Sometimes he will go into such detail in order to get his message across. He speaks slowly and deliberately. His tone can vary from gentle to commanding and is always filled with love. The expression on Blossom's face and her arm and hand movements help to convey his message to you.

The bond of mutual respect White Cloud and Blossom share is one that I would love to experience. It is as if she knows he is always with her. Blossom often queries 'Why Me?' to be the vessel through which White Cloud shares his wisdom. To me, she is eminently qualified through the depth of her own spirituality. She walks her talk with her positive, easy-going nature. Her thoughtfulness, kindness, acceptance of others and generosity of time and service are an example to us all. Blossom and White Cloud share a deeply compassionate nature, an appreciation of others and a humility to which we could all aspire. White Cloud's quirky sense of humour and Blossom's ready laughter make it easy to lift the vibrations.

They are an inspiration to us all. I hope they can influence your life as positively as they have influenced mine

Eileen Stewart
Dip.Tchg; B.Ed;Dip. Counselling; Master NLP Practitioner

INTRODUCTION

Never did I imagine that I would write a book. Yet here I am doing so... for someone else! Someone who has lived many lifetimes on this planet, and now resides in a place we can only dream of.

He asked me if I would commit to writing his words of wisdom into book form, in order for the knowledge he has gained to spread to all those who are willing to learn. How could I refuse?

Allow me to explain. Having been interested in the spiritualist movement since my early twenties, I was told by many a guided soul that I had with me a Native American spirit, there to watch over and protect me. As time progressed, my knowledge grew, and I became interested in healing. I found that whilst working with patients, I was guided to where the healing energy should go, and also, that it seemed to do the trick. During this time I became aware of my Native American guide, not to speak with, or anything as mind boggling as that, just a feeling of gentle security, and a vague image of him in my mind. Once, when healing I asked if I might know his name. Little did I know how two words would become so precious - WHITE CLOUD.

To digress for a moment! For twenty years I had been suffering with a peculiar ailment which neither any kind of doctor or myself could put a name to, and therefore it seemed I had to be suffering from stress! The fact that in general when the symptoms arose, I was feeling positive and on top of the world, did not seem to change their attitude in any way. I saw all kinds of medical whizzes, underwent numerous tests for epilepsy, brain scans, pills, and still nobody could find the answer. I seemed to be experiencing some form of attack, where I would have a series of build up symptoms, followed inevitably by collapsing into a sort of semi coma. Rather unfortunate and at times depending on where I was, rather embarrassing!

Then I met a very gifted clairvoyant. During a 'reading' with her, White Cloud appeared, and I was able to ask him questions. The attacks I was having at the time were getting me down, so I asked what was causing them. The answer was simple. Apparently I would get a build up of healing energy and because it was not being used consistently, it would reach a peak of explosion and conk me out! When I was in the collapsed state, I was aware of everything that was going on, I just couldn't open my eyes or move, to let everybody know I was fine.

In the summer of '99, once again I was suffering with this mystery. The same clairvoyant friend was staying with us and White Cloud kept appearing to her. He was opening and shutting his mouth but was becoming frustrated because he could not be heard. He asked her to ask me if I would get an exercise book and a pen and he would be able to put his words down on paper, through me! At this time in my life, things of this nature were no longer bizarre and so I did as I was asked, feeling rather excited, but also rather ridiculous! No sooner had I opened the book and picked up the pen, words came flooding into my head. He told me he would like me to start a group, named the people he would like to attend, if they wished, and that if it was okay with me, he would like to use me as his channel and actually speak through me.

Now, I had seen people channel before, but I can honestly say, it had never crossed my mind that I might be doing it. A strong feeling of trust and that this was all meant to be enabled me to continue contact with this intriguing new friend. The notebook filled with words of wisdom and encouragement, which I now gladly share with you in the following pages.

On the first meeting, although apprehensive, I knew it would be okay. I had no idea really what to do other than ask for Light and protection around us and 'Over to you White Cloud!' As requested we taped the meetings, which were held on a weekly basis. I was told that the words recorded would become a book and that I was going to write it. How good can things get!

I have been working with White Cloud for four years now and have grown to Love him as my friend and colleague! - as have the souls who have taken the time to listen to him speak. He has so much Love, compassion, wisdom and Truth to share I feel honoured to be part of his work.

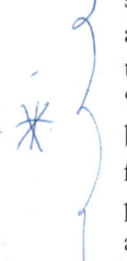

During the meetings, White Cloud asked to see certain souls on a one to one basis and gave them personal guidance according to whatever was happening in their lives at the time. Hence, beyond all imaginings I found myself doing 'readings' for all that heard about him. Eventually, I was told by him that I would have to start charging, not for my gift, but for my time, and before I knew where I was, I had become a professional medium. White Cloud told me that he and I had agreed to do this many moons ago. The 'readings' seemed to be so accurate and guide souls to such a degree, that I soon realised that the gift I had been given was a rare jewel and to be kept polished at all times.

In the time that all this was going on, my partner Goody, son Ritchie and I had applied to emigrate to Australia. We had been fortunate enough to visit and decided that this was where we wanted to be. White Cloud had told us that it was also where we were meant to be. As always he was right, because apart from my partner and I having to get married, which was not really a necessity in our eyes, we sailed through the application, whilst others with far more qualifications, and cash I might add, seemed to be turned down.

So here I am in the merry old Land of Oz. I have arranged to start the meetings and readings over here, and shall see what life brings. I know this book is also 'meant to be', so whatever arrives on these pages as the days unfold, I hope you will enjoy. I hope too that you find wisdom and strength from a wise and Loving Native American spirit named White Cloud, and a middle aged woman who is happy to get his message across on this side of the veil. As for my illness... it disappeared the day I began writing in that little exercise book!

Blossom Goodchild

CHAPTER 1

In this first chapter, White Cloud's manner may seem very formal and the paragraphs disjointed. It is taken from the writings that came through when we first connected. However, in the following chapters when he 'speaks' you will see that he becomes much more user friendly!

WHITE CLOUD: In times gone by, many people looked upon us as holy men, seers, and visionaries. We learnt through nature and compiled our knowledge so it may be used to assist others. The time has come for the mask to be removed. Here lies honesty, purity and an overall desire to be of use in a way that can assist many. From the heavens many descend to spread Light amongst those who are in darkness.

To believe in a God blindly is of little use to the soul - searching, questioning, learning, understanding, using your wisdom and knowledge, this is the pathway to your very being. Knowing your God is different for each of us, for each of us is different, but the 'Truth' of God when found, is a common factor in us all.

If one can get in touch with the 'whole being' of its individual soul, it would be able to function on a level far greater than ever imagined. There is much need for wisdom in your world. Much has been lost or misinterpreted. The Truths of yesterday have been overshadowed by want and greed, but the fact remains that inside each one lies the Truth of the spirit. It is deep rooted in us all. If we are prepared to recover this Truth, then enlightenment shall come.

Your life's path is a way of developing the soul and working out its particular needs. Advancement is created by the self and the desire to grow. How is it that the grass is greener on the other side? This can not be, for one can not escape from the self. To run away is not the answer, but to face your challenges with faith and trust, knowing there is little point in taking an attitude of downcast melancholy. One should except each challenge with joy in the heart, soul and mind, being aware that all can be made less difficult if upliftment of the spirit can occur and spur on the power of positive thinking and creativity. There is no task too difficult, there is no river too deep, for if one has faith and trust, as correctly paraphrased in your world - 'it can move mountains'.

Expect the best in everything. Sometimes we are disappointed and say 'perhaps we expected too much'. Expect the best and you shall have the best! - a much more illuminating way to handle any matter. Sadly there are many souls who are in the darker way of thinking. Not realising or understanding why they are unable to feel peace within themselves. It is a process of encouraging and knowing oneself truly. Knowing that each has the potential inside to be whatever they would like to be and achieve whatever they would like to achieve. All does not have to be bleak, unless you feel unworthy of happiness. So many encounter this entombed emotion. You are what you are, nobody else is the same. What an individual individuality! Express the wonders of your soul. It is not just for some to have it all. It is there waiting for those who are willing to reach out and bring towards them their hearts desires. If all this is done in true Love and faith, for the good and Oneness of all, then there is no reason for this not to come to you.

You have a beautiful day in your world. On this day one can see nature in all its glory. It is so important to recognise this beauty. A happening occurs within the soul self when nature is appreciated. Through this comes understanding.

All life is from the universal life force. All that is 'good' is 'God'. If only souls were to detach themselves from childhood teachings, abolish all doctrines and faiths and find what God is from within themselves. How the Light would shine in their hearts knowing it is 'Their Truth'. For that inner knowledge of the true self when found, brings enlightenment to the understanding of God. Such a simple Truth yet so complex!

Many names are given to this One Power. It matters not what it is called; it matters only that it is found. Many turn away from the Light. With so much war and conflict they can not reason with their Truth. It is important to enlighten those in darkness, but in a manner that can be accepted and understood. It is already beginning, a gradual process. Slowly souls will listen, interest will be sparked by their Inner Light. As the winds of change illumine their inner flame, so too shall their Light become bigger and brighter and we shall give thanks that they have chosen to set themselves on their paths of freedom.

As you are aware in my time on Earth we called God 'The Great Mystery'. Words are inconsequential. It is the emotion and Truth that matter. Allah, Buddha, Jehovah, Great Spirit, Life Force, Universal Energy, Natural law, it is of no importance what one chooses to call it. In our hearts it is the same thing. This is what your people must acknowledge. They should not turn from their hearts desire due to misconception. It is a long and difficult task ahead, but if we can turn only one soul around to find peace, then we have achieved much. To serve the Oneness of the Whole is to serve well.

I would like to speak of gratitude. In all things find reason to give thanks. We blindly accept so many things without realisation of their true source. By giving thanks we are opening up to the many things awaiting us. Taking for granted everyday occurrences is such a widespread dis-ease. If we could only see the upliftment to the Oneness that appreciation brings. It is such a small, easy thing to do, but still we can not find the time. Give thanks and praise with all your hearts, for all things, and you will discover within yourself a new level of energy that this brings. An abundance of joy. It is a never-ending circle of progression.

It is so easy to look upon what is not available. To desire what is not fitting for ones path at that time. Then one looks upon all that others possess and feels envy. Oh how different it could be if everyone appreciated what they have and made full use of it.

It is not the material things of your world that give Love and joy. They are pretty, they can make you feel safe, they ease the toil, but in comparison to all that the soul possesses they have no value at all. There is nothing wrong with achieving material wealth as long as it is kept in its rightful place. The wealth of the soul is something that can not be taken away or broken or lost. It is the surest investment that one could undertake. How rich you are when you have Light in your heart. When this Light encompasses your very being, that Light continues to grow and grow, until you have so much that it is necessary to pass it on to others. As the seed is planted in their souls then they too shall continue to grow in the sunshine of their Inner Light.

Material things are energy, a complex matter but never the less a Truth. The energy can be dispersed. A spiritual energy is of a different nature and where there is Love there is Light.

Betrayal, denial to the soul self is a trait that many encounter. It is so important to contact the Inner self, for here lies all answers. It is not an easy task. It takes much time and meditation. In your world, sadly the rat race never stops. It is run until it can run no more. Never moving anywhere. If only one could see the importance of 'time out'. If they could understand how they would benefit, they perhaps would try a little harder to make the time. Busy, always busy. To what avail? Life is here to be lived. Not to struggle aimlessly, tormenting body and soul with responsibilities and commitments. Relax, let go, enjoy the moment. So few have accomplished this. How sad this is. Encourage oneself to 'BE'. It can lift the energies of the Whole. It could make such a difference to your planet Earth. How it struggles to show its beauty, when it is being destroyed from every corner inwards. To treasure your Mother Earth would change many things. It is not too late, but I must stress that time is running short. Spread the message of Love, for this and only this can be the saving factor.

All will change and the New World will be as the world once was long ago. There shall be much repenting, but then it would be too late. What is done is done. If your world could start now by respecting nature as part of the Universal Life Force, by giving it thought as one would the soul, what a magnitudinal effect this could have on all things. Try to get in touch with the self on the deepest level, for the deeper the seed is sown the more chance it has of survival.

In our world there is no time, just continuum of the soul spirit. Let it grow. Have deeper commitment to the true self. Why should you fear the Truth? It is so simple. Believe, trust and know that in His complete Love there can never be failure. In His complete wisdom there can never be a lack of understanding. For the Oneness we know as God is forever giving, forever willing to bring his children home. Once they can allow the God within to find its true origin, then and only then may the soul find the Light in which to follow, in which to feel safe and Loved, comforted and warm. Then and only then may the soul find its home, within its own heart. How we praise and exalt when such a triumphant happening occurs for one more child that was lost has been found and returned safely home.

Oh how we weep to see all the injustice of your world. Man has become blind. He walks his path blinkered, looking always straight ahead, never taking in the view around him, in its entirety. What is missed? What glories and wonders are passed by unnoticed?

We must all unite in our power and Love, to create harmony and peace. Being an example to those who are angry and tormented. Being a haven for those who have nowhere to belong. To give Love to these souls will be of great fortitude for their existence on Earth at this time. We all have our chosen paths. Remember free will. It is vital.

'Choice' is the giver and the receiver; it is the wrong and the right. It is YOU. You alone can decide your destiny. If you chose to follow the path of the right, (that is the right within yourself) then truly you are on the path of good, bringing into your life only good. If you should choose otherwise, then so be it. The road shall become longer and harder, but never the less, each of God's children shall return home to Him. A shepherd does not desert his flock. He watches over them. They are his family. Should the Mother/Father of all good desert the flock? Why it could not be so.

For LOVE is what GOD IS.
LOVE means GOD.
GOD means LOVE.
It is one and the same.

'*' 'Feeling' pure, unconditioual LOVE

CHAPTER 2

Our meetings began in September 99. I was unable to record the first few. The following pages are recorded words from White Cloud. His wisdom spoken as gently as the evening breeze. His Love given unconditionally.
I have included some personal questions asked at the meetings as I feel the answers may be beneficial to many.

WHITE CLOUD: Good evening to you my fine friends.

Truth. I would like to speak to you of your Truth. Your personal Truth. It is a Truth that is directed automatically with the Divine Oneness. It matters not the Truth of the person sitting next to you or the Truth of the person in your supermarket. It matters not at all of anybody else's Truth other than your own. There are times in your lives when you are confused by your own Truths. You sit and you ponder about what it is you are really feeling. It is by sitting and pondering that you are able to go inside your soul and truly discover what it is you are searching for. You will find inevitably that you are searching for your own Truth. You may ask questions. You may find the same question in a book with an answer to it. You may ask a friend a question and that friend would give you an answer, but it does not necessarily mean that it is the answer you are looking for. The answer you are looking for is deep within your soul. It is a question of learning. For this my dearest friends, is why we are here. We choose to return time after time to learn what we have not yet learnt. As you are probably aware, when you are in 'spirit' you have discussions with elders, wiser than you, as to your purpose on your return. It is important indeed the exact time you are born, where you are born and to whom you are born. These matters have been discussed in great detail with you.

Sometimes when you look at a newborn child, it is as if he

has his old face from his lifetime before. For he looks rather old and wrinkled. As one progresses in this world the age will disappear from that young baby. He has forgotten why he has actually returned. During a lifetime of a soul there are many lessons brought to them in order to learn the reasons they returned. This soul may choose to ignore the opportunities that are brought its way in order to learn knowledge for its soul to grow and expand. You are here to learn and to Love. It is as simple and yet as complicated as that. As you learn so you Love.

When these opportunities come your way, if you take advantage of them, then a deeper understanding grows within your soul. If you choose perhaps at a particular time not to take advantage, then it does not mean that you will not be given an opportunity at a later date. Unaware to you, you are simply prolonging the process.

There are many reasons why you have chosen to come into the particular place that you did. There are many questions sometimes as to why you did. At times it seems to make no sense. Whoever you may come across within your life span this time round, whoever it may be, and for however little or large amount of time spent with those people, understand that each soul that you communicate with is there to raise your vibration of learning. Some souls you may well feel totally at ease with. You enjoy spending much time in their company. This makes you feel Loved. It makes you feel warm. It is a wonderment to feel so Loved and so at ease among such friends. I would like to say this also, it is time spent amongst souls that you do not feel so at ease with that is probably more of a learning experience. Then you have to put into practice many things that lay deep inside your soul. It could well be that you do not feel comfortable with these people, or a certain person, because of a past lifetime. It may well be, that whatever took place in a past lifetime is now to be resolved. It may not be that case at all. It may be purely that within your plan of your particular life, that you have been guided to meet with a particular soul, because that soul has been put there to stir things up inside of you, to make you ask certain questions about yourself and indeed about others. So do bear that in mind if you would. It is not always the people you feel most comfortable with that are helping you to learn your lessons. If perhaps you could look upon the people you feel ill at ease with, knowing that actually they are doing you a rather large favour, then maybe your feelings towards them will change and their feelings towards you will change, and an occurrence will take place that will raise the energies of both those particular souls.

Throughout your lives my friends, you will be faced with new challenges. Take one step at a time. Take each step slowly and you will be in balance. It is like a young child when it is learning to walk. There are many times when it stumbles and falls. With a young child, unless they have hurt themselves, they will get up, brush themselves down and try again. They will continue with this effort because they are aware that if they keep on trying they will eventually achieve the task they are aiming for. There will be times when you fall and times when you hurt yourself. They will not be lifelong scars. They will merely be, as a child, sitting there for a little while in order to recover. When you feel ready to stand again, indeed you shall do so. Next time you will take a little more care with your step. You will balance out your body to make sure that you go straight and that you do not topple over.

I feel it is now my favourite time of the evening, when we may enjoy ourselves and allow interplay with each other in conversation. Is there anybody that would care to start this evening?

A question was then asked regarding crystals and their energies.

An incident had arisen regarding the possibilities of negative energy within these gems. The lady who inquired uses crystals for personal healing.

I am aware of which you speak. Indeed there are energies that are able to incase themselves within each crystal. These crystals are from deep within the ground. They hold many, many healing powers, for they have been around for a very long time. Some of these crystals may perhaps get into the wrong hands and darker energies may be infused inside of them. There are many ways to cleanse a crystal of these... I don't like to use the word bad energies, but perhaps, lesser Light energies. I do feel crystals are a very important part of your healing, but this does not come from anybody else other than yourself. The more you are to attune yourself to these crystals, the clearer things shall become. It is a case of sitting down, holding your crystal to your heart and to your head, and the two will enable you to connect as to how they may benefit you. Your oils that you have, they too are a gift that you should elaborate on. You need to tune into these oils within your crystals. By putting certain oils onto certain crystals, you can create a reaction. It is important for you to then put these crystals where your pain is. Once you have done this, then you use your own healing power, because the connection through your mind, into the creation that you have caused on these crystals, will work with each other. It is like a telephone wire that you have in your sky. Imagine that from here *(arm gestures)*, to wherever you have placed your crystals is a complete healing energy. Understand it is initially coming from here *(heart)* it is going up here *(head)* to heal your mind. It is going to wherever you need to place that crystal to take away the problem that is causing you pain. If you would allow yourself to do this at least every other day, you would be aware of the difference it is making and also my dear friend you would feel happier inside because it is you that is doing your own healing. Do you understand? Thank you. Are there any other questions?

Three of us present here, have been helping the lady with healing, are we to continue this or will she do her own healing?

Let me explain this. One thought from my friends in this room, be it from someone who does not even know our friend, one moment of thought toward helping this lady to get better, works within the energy to make her better. It is obviously an important thing, that when any one of you are able to give your thought or spend time with your healing, then by all means continue and continue, because the power then will be recharged. It is like a battery, if you overwork it and do not let it charge up, it will run down and go flat. So therefore when it comes to recharging, it takes a great deal of energy and a great deal of time. Whereas if you continue on a level where all the time you are topping up this healing energy it makes less work for all concerned. I would like to say also that the three that have been working with our friend, the particular energy that the three of you have, works very well together. It is the triangle. The three types of energy being used, make it a particularly strong one. I would ask, if it be your wish and your desire, that it would be very beneficial to do this work with her as often as you are able. I realise there is a matter of trust within this whole... I would like to say...paraphernalia. I am also aware of the hearts and souls of all those involved. Where your desire is true, your trust is strengthened. It shall take place, but as to the time limit, that is indeed up to each and every one of you. It is also quite a good idea when the healing is taking place, if it is not possible for others to be present, then a few of your calls on your dialling system to those that are aware would help. If other friends are able at that time to tune into the healing energy that is taking place a much greater amount of energy is built up and it is able to come into the whole situation and shall benefit our friend greatly. So, to cut a long story short! Yes, it is imperative that this healing continues.

My friends. It is time now for me to take my leave.

We give thanks to the Divine Oneness for allowing this meeting to take place. We ask always that we may remain humble in order to serve and that we may continue to walk in the Light and the Love.

Adieu, my friends, Adieu.

CHAPTER 3

WHITE CLOUD: Good evening to you my dearest friends.

I would like to start by speaking with you of snowdrops. Picture, if you would, these tiny little flowers. The purity of their colour - the colour of the snow. They are so small, but just because they are small does not mean that they go unnoticed. Indeed, when one is walking by, one would stop and wonder at their beauty. What I would like to say, is that no matter how small something may be, no matter how it feels, insignificant because of its minuteness, this does not mean that it should be passed unnoticed. You may feel that sometimes you do a deed of kindness for a friend and it maybe of such little consequence to you, but it is not so to the person receiving that giving. When you have a bunch of snowdrops all together you are able to look at them and all around you see their beauty, because together, when they are all in a bunch, they become more noticeable. As you do small deeds and your friends help others in turn, then these small deeds become noticed. Each small deed that is performed means so much. It is important that these little acts are given freely through the heart.

There was then a VERY long pause.

Please do not be of concern with the silence. There is reasoning in all things.

Another VERY long pause.

I wonder how many of you, during that silence, thought about what somebody else might have been thinking within that silence? I wonder if any of you felt a little uncomfortable? I would ask you to consider that sometimes when one is within a group of people you may feel a little uneasy. Have you ever considered that the other people in the room might too be feeling uneasy? Felt a little concern as to what is going to be said next? Or who is going to say it? It is here that I would like you to think about the gift of speech. The gift of giving kind words to those who are shy perhaps or those who are nervous. Look inside your heart and you will know that if you just give a little extra Love, if you could break that silence, you could make those around you less shy, less nervous, you could make them feel at home. All it takes is one sentence. Something very small perhaps. It matters not what you say. What matters is to give your Love to these people who do not feel that they have a home anywhere on this Earth. Many of us have these places of secure homes. Many of us are able to finish our daily duties and come back to a place that is home. Walls that surround you with Love. Walls where you want to be.

Sometimes, although it is somebody's home, it may not be full of Love when they get there. It may not make them feel easy and comfortable and therefore within their heart they once again feel this loss. Thus looking for somewhere to feel safe. What I would like to say is that nobody really needs walls to feel safe. They need people to make them feel secure. They need Love. That is all they need in order to have a home.

Consider the snail. It carries its home on its back. Wherever it feels like stopping, it can stop, it can pull itself up into its little shell and feel safe there until it is ready to move on. This is the way it should be my friends. That wherever you are you would be able to stop and feel at home. It is important also that wherever you may stop on your pathway through life that you may feel safe and warm within the home that you have placed yourself. This is such a simple thing. People do not realise. They fail to understand the power of speech. How it can make one feel safe. It does not take very much. It takes very little, but my goodness!, how it can make one feel as if they are sitting amongst a field of snowdrops. When the snow comes down and covers these snowdrops, it matters not that the snow is cold, because these little things that people do make the heart warm, no matter what is falling down! I ask if you would keep this in mind. It may be someone that you are interacting with in your shop or your supermarket. It maybe somebody crossing the road. It takes not more than a few seconds to smile and ask how they are. Even if you do not know them, a little 'Hello, how are you?' might make somebody feel Loved. You might be unaware of their situation. It might just be that that person has not had a soul inquire after their well-being for a very long time. This little thing to them, can make them feel they are worth while. If more and more would think just to ask of the well being of another. Not to ask on the flippant wavelength, but ask from the heart and mean it. You see, so much in your world is just said and means nothing. If it is Love based and expressed in this fashion, what a difference it can make.

I would like to speak also of the listening. Sometimes you might ask after a person's health. They might reply in a way that you really do not feel you have time for today. It is important to take the time. It is important, if somebody needs to release these darker clouds that have overshadowed them. For this is very healing and all it takes is this *(touches mouth)* to be put to work, and this, connected to this *(touches ear)*. You have a song in your world about a skeleton I believe. About a knee bone connected to the thighbone and all this sort of paraphernalia. Indeed if you think about it, these things *(ear and mouth)* are connected for reason. All these things work at their fullest when they are led by the heart.

It is becoming very close to a very special time of the year. This is a time when people join together. It is a time when people send little square pieces of paper to one another. Perhaps people they have not spoken to since the last time they sent that little piece of paper. It might say on that little piece of paper exactly the same thing as it said last time you sent it. This really does not matter. I suppose it is the thought that counts. My friends, take time to think when you are writing with these little cards, just take time to put your Love into them. This Yuletide that is coming upon us is indeed a very special time. It is a very happy time for some, but it is a very lonely time for others. It would not hurt anyone of the souls that walk your path, just to send Light to all those who really can not bear the thought of this Christmas time that is coming around. For many feel so alone. So please, when you have a few minutes to yourself, send out your thoughts and your Love to those who are not as fortunate as yourself. These things do make such a vast difference. They raise the energies of the lonely.

Here we are again at my favourite time. First of all my apologies. I have not welcomed into the group a young man who unbeknown to you I have watched over many a time. I welcome and I am very pleased to have you with us this evening. Who would like to go first?

My question is mainly about Love, but to do with partners and soul mates and whether one has a particular soul mate or many?

When a man and a woman come together in an Earthly situation, there are many, many sections of Love. You cannot put Love into any form of category. Many people spend their Earthly lifetime with a partner that indeed they Love dearly and from the very depth of their heart. They care without doubt for this person that they have shared their life with. This does not necessarily mean that is their soul partner. A soul mate as you call them. This is a very complex matter. The soul comes from a group. You may come across a soul from within your group that fills you in your heart. You say 'This must definitely be my soul mate'. I am aware of many people that feel this, but this is not necessarily the case. Look at the word 'soul mate.' If they are a friend, they are a part of your soul group. So they are in that sense, very close to your heart. This is why one feels this very close connection. To go into the matter of 'soul mate' in the way people interpret it in your Earth life, goes into reason that at this time is far too complicated. There are many, many issues surrounding this. There are many different souls. If I may say, it is again a matter that needs to be gone into in greater depth. If I were to begin to explain now, I would not be able to make myself clear. I am aware and I have said before, of certain matters that would need an entire evening to explain. One would need almost a notebook and calculator to sort these matters out. It is a matter that, being where you are, is not necessarily comprehensible from your viewpoint. I would indeed like to try again at another time, as I would some other matters that have arisen. Is this acceptable? I feel I have left you in the dark rather.

This was acceptable!

May I ask as to whether you can be in more than one place at a time?

Oh yes, yes! This is again a matter of there being the time. Everything within the spiritual dimension from where we are is very, very different. May I say that although this is acceptable to us, it is also, if you are able to comprehend, an easy possibility for each and every one of you to be as well. It is again one of those things that has been shut down. Please understand that there are souls that are living on your Earth plane that are able to do this. They are able to sit there at dinner and have a conversation with Mr. and Mrs. Smith and they are also able to be on the other side of the world having a swim in the Indian Ocean! It is just a matter of allowing your knowledge and your wisdom to be expressed and allowing the soul to reach its fullest awareness. As I have said, unfortunately long, long ago these things were shut down. There will come a time, it is difficult to say when, because of course it depends upon the attunement of the souls that are to be living and dwelling in the times ahead, that this will be able to be in your world, a part of every day living

There were no more questions.

Then if I may I would like to bring this evening to a close. Once again I would like to thank all of you for taking the time to come and listen to the words that I have to say. I realise that they are not of any great intelligence, if you like, but it is not intelligence that makes the world go round, it is Love. As pure and as simple as that. These simple scenarios, that I am able to pass onto you, are the things that matter, not how the workings of stars and things around the universe are taking place. Although I totally accept that there are those who find interest in that. It is their future, but may I say, within all things, within every day living, do not make things so complicated, then they become knotted up inside yourself. They are unable to be of value. Think always of the simplicity. Think always of Loving, and Living, and Learning.

We thank The Great Spirit for allowing these evenings to take place. We give thanks also for all the wonders that are purveyed. May we continue to receive our blessings, that we may be forever walking towards the Light and the nearer we become the brighter the Light shall shine upon us all.

Adieu, my friends Adieu.

CHAPTER 4

WHITE CLOUD: Greetings to you all my dear friends. I welcome our new friends that have joined us this evening.

I am aware of the subject that we have agreed to speak of this evening. I would like to say, have you got your pen and paper at hand because this can be a very complex matter!

There is an exact time for each individual soul to descend upon this Earth and there is an exact time for that soul to arise from this Earth to return home. There are certain circumstances that can change an individual's length of time, but this is indeed a rarity. With most souls they depart at their appointed time. In your world people express their sorrow over an accident. Keep that word 'accident' at the forefront of your mind because I shall refer back to it. For instance, the passing that takes place, say, with a small child being hit by an automobile. If the time is ready for that child to 'go home' then nothing and nobody can put a stop to this. That child had learnt all that was necessary for that child to return for. Sometimes when a young baby is taken back to 'his true home' it leaves the parents very sad. This baby has chosen to do this, not necessarily for what that soul had to learn, but to give its parents a helping hand in the things that they had returned to learn.

So you see in these ways of your world, when your people say 'How can there be a God if He lets starving children in another of your countries die?' This is not so. They have chosen to be born in that particular place and time for many reasons. It could be their lesson is to be a short one. It could be as a soul group that they have offered to come down so that they can show others a way of giving. They are prepared to sacrifice and give their Love through pain to show others the way.

Now, when children return 'home', they have not been detached for long from their natural spiritual self. So there are different circumstances with these little ones. A little soul is never afraid upon death. They would find themselves in a place that we like to call 'The Summerland'. Some have sadly been very damaged. These little ones are within a certain group. They need special attention to repair their depleted souls. It is perhaps as your buildings of caring that you have in your world. Other little ones are playing most of the time. If a soul was able to see the joy that is within the children's Summerland, ones heart would be immediately lifted. The laughter from these children is so pure and unharmed. Souls from our realms, when doing repair work on other grown developed souls might take them to the Summerland, because it is a place of great healing and great joy.

I would like to speak now of what is known as the 'silver cord'. There is an ethereal cord that is attached to the soul. It is that cord that enables the soul, the spirit, to remain inside the flesh. Upon the passing from this plane to the other, it is only able to take place when the silver cord is cut. This allows the soul to be released from the flesh in order to return 'home.' This is where it becomes very complicated. You see my friends, it depends entirely upon the growth and development of the spirit as to how and where they arrive on their journey to the new lands. May I start perhaps with a soul that felt it an unnecessary thing to know of a life force of goodness. A soul that perhaps chose to live life in darkness. Their Light on this Earth plane was darker because they were unaware. If they chose to believe that when the flesh is no longer activated, there is nothing, then sadly when their cord has been cut, they find themselves in a place of confusion. They are unable to accept that they are, I paraphrase 'dead'. They had always felt that when this moment came they would simply be no more. On arriving in the other world they can not comprehend where they are. Their circumstance of passing will also affect where they arrive. Many people in your world who have encountered a 'near death' experience have spoken of the tunnel with the Light at the end. This is not necessarily an event that happens within every individual case, but indeed to many this may occur. It does not matter if you arrive at the end of your journey by going through the tunnel. You see in your world, if you want to get from A to B, some of you take a train, some of you take an automobile and others may walk. So you see for each particular soul there could be many different ways of arriving into the other realms.

I would go back now to a soul who had no knowledge of an after life. There are so many, many cases because you see we are all individual. For those who are unaware it would be that, perhaps firstly a loved one would appear to them and souls that perhaps they are familiar with that have passed on, in order to make them feel secure and in order to make the connection of 'the other side'. For that individual knows that the souls it is seeing 'died'. In other cases it might be that a soul from higher realms who has chosen to work with the lost soul that has newly arrived, has come down to help them understand and evolve. It would be like an immediate friendship. It might take this individual to many places. To show certain things that the soul needs to understand to accept where it is now. This is where we could talk for a thousand years. When I say 'take this soul to many places' in fact, that soul is on the same spot. Your mind, your soul, your spirit are no longer restricted. You are able, and this I understand is not something that is easily comprehensible, you are able to have in front of you, exactly when you need it, what is necessary for your soul's growth.

You have choices all along. Some souls believe it or not, prefer to think that they are still 'alive'. They had not done the preparation before hand. This is when you in your realm, your Earthly plane, are able to see those who have passed on in their physical form. That soul has not been able to release the imagination. It still feels that it must have this physical attachment and so it makes itself attached to its old physical flesh. With these souls, there will always come a time when either a particular soul from the higher realms is able to offer help or indeed a soul from your plane. At the end of the day, it is only when that individual is ready to accept its path that it shall be able to move on.

As when you are on your Earth, you recognise points in your lifetime where you are able to look back and you realise that you have developed and grown. This is no different in the other realms. We are always working to move towards the Great Light, as indeed I still am, and there is a long way to go.

Souls choose to return to your Earth, not because they do not like it elsewhere but because there is such a development of the soul. The lessons are hard and they are tough. They challenge you to the very core. This is what you are aware of. You realise that you would like to develop certain things within your soul and by returning to the Earth plane this is the quickest way of doing so.

On the planes above, 'life' if I may call it that, never dies. For souls that are aware of the Light and have learned their lessons well and accomplished their reasons for returning, the Light is with them immediately when their cord is cut. They have this sense of well being because they have returned safely. From then on they continue. There is no change within the soul from the moment one is lying on the Earth plane... one moment while the cord is cut... and then your soul is on a different plane, that is all. The Light is clearer. Your understanding is clearer. Your spiritual eyes are clearer. Your heart, where your soul and spirit reside, is free from any attachment that bore down upon the soul because of physical ailments. Once you are in a position to rest for a while, merely enjoy the beauty. May I say it is a beauty beyond compare. For with your human eyesight you are unable to minutely envisage the wonders of the heavens. Perhaps when you have rested, it is entirely your choice, you will be sent a guide who will be there to assist you on your path. There are many, many, many possibilities for you to choose and this is such an expanse that I could not possibly name them all. The work of Light continues on. If you are already working with the Light on the Earth plane, then it is mostly accepted that this work will continue. It may be to help souls to work with children. It may be to work with souls who simply do not wish to progress because of a loved one that resides still on the Earth plane and is unable to accept and move on because of the Love attachment. There are so many wonderful works.

Are there any questions that would like to be arisen concerning the area we have spoken of?

Can a soul make a choice about whether to come back to learn more lessons on this Earth plane or not? Is that something that the soul has no choice about? Do they know they must do it? Would the soul know that they have to finish these lessons and come back, or whether they can make a choice?

Yes, you see, when a soul is of the higher planes, it has an overall understanding and a need for quality that it has not yet allowed itself to receive. It is a question of not necessarily wanting to return. It is rather a poor place compared with the realms of other souls. It becomes a wanting because of the understanding of where one wants to get to. It is never a decision made entirely by the individual. There is a council of higher souls who will always give advice, knowledge and wisdom as to the particular reasons one is to return. To give guidance as to the particular place, time, planet, parents etc. Many aspects are taken into consideration. It may be that the soul being advised is not happy to return, purely because it is aware of the fact that once it has returned it will lose the knowledge and wisdom of the pathway it is to walk. It is aware of the many, many challenges that the Earth life can put upon a soul. But it would return knowing that at the end of that journey it had gained what it needed. Knowing also the knowledge of free choice. May I quickly add that when you are on the Earth plane, you have the free choice to turn your circumstances around. You have that knowledge everyday. It does not mean that if a certain message has to be learned that may be harsh to the soul perhaps, that that soul has to have a harsh life. We all know there is choice and if we have choice we can choose which way we learn.

It is time now my dearest friends for me to take my leave.

We give thanks to the Divine Oneness for allowing this meeting to take place. We ask always that we may remain humble in order to serve and that we may continue to walk in the Light and the Love.

Adieu my friends. Adieu.

CHAPTER 5

WHITE CLOUD: A very good evening to you my friends.

Take time my dearest friends, every day, to listen to what your hearts have to say. The hubbub that is around you does not allow for the silence that is needed to keep at peace with ones mind, soul and body. It is essential to your well being for these three to be at one with each other. It takes but a little time and it will make a vast difference to the balance that you are able to maintain.

When one is out of sorts and all is not in alignment, you would be quite surprised at the difference that this can make as to the way you are behaving, feeling and conducting yourself. If when you are able to take this time out, for even just a short period, it would be beneficial to you to visualise the energy field that encompasses you - to imagine that it is intact - that there is a golden Light surrounding the colours that you are able to see. This Light could keep the aura protected and prevent negativity or alien energies protruding into your personal space.

I am showing to Blossom a golden chalice. You are to drink from this chalice and imagine that the liquid you are swallowing is pure from the Divine river source. It is filling your body with the strength, Love and energy that is needed for you to go ahead and work with the elements that are now being brought to you. This liquid can be your inner protection. It will fill you with an excitement and a source of power that feels new to you. When you are feeling a little depleted, imagine, if you would, taking a drink from the golden chalice. Always before drinking I ask for you to give thanks for the gifts you are receiving.

At this point in the meeting, the link suddenly was lost, and we could not get back in contact. The following day I decided to 'tune in' by myself, to see if I could find out what had happened.

My loved one. It is a joy to speak with you and be with you, just ourselves.

The reasoning behind my abrupt departure last evening is due to the fact that the time was not the correct time for me. You were able to see me in my robes of white. There is a ceremony within our world that is of importance. There is sadness within my soul, for this ceremony was of that nature. We are able, in certain circumstances, to bring a soul further into the Light. But there is a dramatic pull from the realms of a darker nature and when a soul is seeking help, there is much Light energy required to transform this soul from the darkness it had once chosen to reside in.

Again at this point the link was lost. I was left a little confused but have learned as time has passed that it is not always possible due to mixed energies for all to go smoothly. I sometimes used to feel that it was me and perhaps I was at fault, but I know now that this is not the case.

Many aspects are involved for White Cloud when uniting his energies with mine. Most of them I have no knowledge of at all. This is not through choice but perhaps beyond my comprehension. I have learned to accept this as my understanding broadens.

CHAPTER 6

WHITE CLOUD: Good evening to you my friends.

How the songs of the birds uplift the soul and the air of spring comes upon ones heart. Uplift your souls my friends, for there is much excitement in the air. There is electricity around you all. It is sending out waves that shall reach far beyond that which you imagine your capabilities to be. These waves shall reach souls who shall be visiting you from many miles away. Look back on how I once spoke of things taking place that were beyond your imaginings. Look individually amongst yourselves and can you honestly say, you have not progressed a long, long way. You have all moved upwards and onwards according to the pace that you individually are able to contend with.

You will find that within this year of the millennium that much shall take place to the point of sitting back in your chairs with open mouths in total amazement. Your hearts shall be filled with joy also.

There is so much that is on offer. There are so many opportunities. It would be very rewarding if you were able to make other souls aware of these attributes that are out there for one and all. It is, as I have said in the past, a difficult task to bring these souls to this state of awareness. Where there is a will there is a way. It is as if each one of you is a beacon, and people are attracted to this. They shall be encouraged by your example.

There was then a change in energy and I wasn't really sure what was about to occur. After a time I realised that White Cloud wanted to open my eyes and see through mine. It was a very peculiar experience as when this happened I felt as if my eyes were bulging out of their sockets. They were unable to look around, but none the less see through my eyes is what he did. Please take note that later on in this book, as we progressed in working with each other, White Cloud has been able to accomplish this to the degree of looking into peoples eyes and chatting as if in the room.

I thank you for your thoughts. I have just achieved something that I was experimenting with. I was able to open the eyes of Blossom and see for myself the view through her eyes. I am very excited now. I do apologise if I worried you in any way. It was merely a question of the transference of vibration in order to try and achieve what I was aiming for. Unfortunately I had not made that very clear to my friend Blossom! This is a way of relaying to you that anything is possible should you have the necessary desire to achieve something. I feel the force of the energy that you are sending to me and I appreciate your Love and kindness. My friends, I may appear to have been very selfish this evening. It is part of my future plans with my friend Blossom and it was merely a question of moving a little further within our bonding. I apologise if you found this worrying or offensive in any manner. From the mischievous side of my heart I shall be able to dance with glee, because I have been working towards this for some time. I give thanks to the energies you sent me in order for such an accomplishment to take place.

We give thanks to the Divine Oneness for allowing this meeting to take place. We ask always that we may remain humble in order to serve and that we may continue to walk in the Light and the Love.

Adieu, my friends, Adieu.

CHAPTER 7

WHITE CLOUD. A very good evening to you. It feels a long time since we have all been gathered.

Do not despair in the privacy of your inner thoughts, there must always be hope, for where there is hope there is always Light. However small your thoughts of hope, however tiny your flickering Light, there is always room for expansion. Hope brings Hope. It is a very easy thing to allow the negative energies to penetrate ones mind when ones body is feeling at a low ebb. This my dearest ones is the time for you to hold on with all your might to what you know to be your Truth. Allow the angels and all that is good to surround your very being, then think no more. Allow the Love that is being given to you to penetrate through to the very depths of your souls. Drink in this Love and let it fill your entire being. There is around each individual that walks this planet of yours, angels, guides, friends and helpers. They have made it their responsibility to be with you and walk in your steps. There are times, if you allow your spirit to open up, that you can almost physically feel their Love. There are also times when it is as if you have built a wall around yourself that makes it very difficult for your loving spirit aids to penetrate through. This does not mean that they are not there. They are always there for you. There are times also when it is more fortuitous for the individual soul to walk the pathway as if they are on their own. They have to learn the lessons that they have come here to learn. It is then that these angels and friends unhappily have to take a step back and allow your soul to grow. This does not mean that they do not weep with you when you weep. It would just not be beneficial at this time for them to draw too close.

Understand this my friends that with every footstep you walk towards the Light, then the Light within your soul is illuminated just that little bit more. There is a saying in your world that sometimes you seem to take three steps forward and five back, then it seems that you only take another two forward so you are somehow still behind. There is reason in all things. Perhaps when you walked the three steps forward you did not quite take in the full quality of step number two. You needed to recede and walk these steps once more with a little more care, a little more respect and a little more thought. For there would be little point in leaping forward on your pathway if you had not trodden the stairwell very carefully. At times ones every day living can become an enormous weight upon ones shoulders. It becomes a drudgery. It feels as if one is looking for pastures new. It is during this drudgery that you find your inner strength. You learn your lessons more deeply and more solidly. There is no question, my dear friends in the fact that as low as one can feel, in all things there are opposites. Without doubt when the time is correct for that particular soul, it shall reach the heights and they are higher than the previous time. In so speaking one will at another point become lower than perhaps ever before. Look upon this as a mere process for the soul. Know through these darker times that the clouds shall roll away and the sun shall shine so brightly once again. Then as time emerges and ones soul becomes in true balance with itself, the lows shall never again become so low, but the highs when the soul has reached a certain maturity shall continue to rise.

Take, if you will, an image of ducks on a pond. They glide through the water and they create ripples that spread outwards. This does not take much effort for the motion with their feet is a natural one which causes these ripples to expand. Look upon the Love in your heart as a natural one. With no effort at all allow the ripples of Love to exude from your hearts and spread so easily towards others. It takes not a moments effort to send Love. The work that is then put into play by the Divine Force becomes an enormity that can reach far afield.

Love, as I have said many a time, is the key my friends. When one is feeling at a loss, simply repeat over and over, Love, Love, Love. For this without fail shall raise the vibration within your energy field and Lighten your load.

It is permissible now for any questions and as you are aware this is my favourite time of the evening.

In a previous meeting you were able to see through Blossom's eyes. Is this something you can do more frequently now or was it a one off sensation for you?

The pleasure that it gave to me uplifted my soul and my purpose. It was the most wondrous thing for me to have achieved. I might say I was like a child after that. I was heralding the news to one and all. The energy this took from Blossom, unaware to her quite how much, was something for me to take note off. It certainly would not be something that I do all the time. It is something that is the beginning of many phenomenal aspects to do with the work that Blossom and I have chosen to do. This will be brought to Light in future times. As we work together we are able to become more attuned to each other's energy. As it is for me now, there is a vibrational level that I am able to use in order to speak as I am doing. If I was to project a voltage stronger than Blossom's energy field is accustomed to, it could do her temporary harm. This I would not wish. So it is I trust in time, that little by little, I am able to turn up the voltage on our vibrational fields in order for us to fuse together more and more as time allows. Of course it would be entirely Blossom's decision as to how much voltage she will allow me to integrate. I am more than happy with the volume and the level that we are attuned to at this point in our work together. I must stress once again of the utter joy for me to be able to view through human eyes after such a long, long time. We do not need eyes in the world of the heavens. We do not require anything other than love.

My friends it is so wonderful for me to be able to communicate with you in this manner. I trust you have as much enjoyment from these gatherings as myself. I am aware that the love I send to you is reciprocated.

May we always go forth in the knowledge that the Divine Oneness is with us at all times. May we never cease to give thanks and praise for the wonders of our very being.

Until our next meeting I give you my humble thanks.

Adieu, my friends, Adieu.

CHAPTER 8

For several meetings we were unable to connect with the White Cloud energy. I was concerned that this might have been some failing on my part, White Cloud was quick to alleviate this fear.

WHITE CLOUD. Welcome to you my friends.

I am very excited that we are once again united. It is a pleasure to be back with you. I have been away concerning other important matters that could not be disregarded and needed the requirement of my entire energy. There has been nothing and there never will be any fault or wrong doing on your parts, but due to the intensity of the dilemma to which I was called it was best for me to leave things be. I know in your hearts you knew truth of this. There comes with me a white dove of peace. You may recall I have spoken before concerning a bird in flight. It may be this time, when you allow the wind current to position itself accurately beneath your wings, that there is no work required by you other than to be taken along to where your next destination lies.

I am aware of the marvellous news regarding Blossom and Mr Goody's move across to the land of the rock. Sadly this will mean that this little group shall disperse but true friendship never dies. You know I would never desert friends. Because the lady whom I use as my channelling instrument will no longer be with you in person, this does not mean that you will not be able to communicate with me. Do you think that my warriors that were with me from the beginning shall be suddenly dropped in my project? I do not think so.

There is much transformation taking place within you all. You are aware on the surface of such movement. It is impossible for you to understand the transformation that is taking place on your deeper spiritual level. You have been trapped inside your cocoon and the time has arrived for you to shed your shell and to immerge into a beautiful butterfly. But... butterflies have wings you know and these wings need to be used. When a butterfly perches on a flower for instance, somebody viewing the beauty of the two together can find much solace in the stillness of the two being united as one picture. Allow for souls to see the picture you present in all your beauty. Beauty that stems from within. One must dig deep sometimes because we allow a lot of earth to hide what has been buried for a long time. It is merely a question of dispersing all the soil as you dig and leaving the ground open to discover your hidden buried treasure.

I am showing a picture of myself dancing around a campfire at night. This was a ritual we performed for many different reasons. This particular ceremony is in honour for when we lived on your Earth. We were able to respect all things of living nature. We would give thanks to the Great Mystery and honour things of nature and give thanks for them. It would help your souls to grow if you took a little time to offer your thanks in honour of the beauty you see around you. Many things I have already spoken of in a different manner. To you these may seem simple things that you feel you know. May I ask how often you put this into play? The more you become aware of Divine beauty and workings and give thanks, the more you will be able to understand.

I am showing to Blossom a yellow canary. The bird has its claws on its perch and has now slipped completely underneath as if it is hanging upside down. The claws are still in the same place where it has rooted its foundational grasp. Sometimes you may feel full of song and life and exuberance then as quick as a flash, for no reason, you feel as if your world is upside down. Know that if your roots are firmly planted in your soul then you can never fall off your perch! There is a cage in which this canary is living. The door has always been open but the canary has never sought to look. It has seen the outside of the cage but has not known how to get there. There are many ups and downs before one is able to leave the cage. For a while it may sit on the bottom amongst the debris and the mess. It may feel it has not the strength to reach the side where it can see the open door. Strength is always within. It takes but a leap of faith. As the canary finds itself at the edge of the cage, should it attempt to fly out having not done so before? It knows not whether it shall fall. It also knows that the answer cannot be found until it tries. It takes that leap, not only does it find it can fly in much more space, it flies straight to an open window. From there it can soar into the blue sky into a vast world that up until now it did not know existed. Set yourself free, my friends, from your cages. You are aware of the world outside your cage and how exciting it would be to enter that world. You have no idea of the worlds that can be entered after that. There is no end to your growth and knowledge.

We naturally give our Love and thanks to the Divine Oneness that is in all. May we always serve in Love and Light.

Until next time my friends I bid you Adieu.

CHAPTER 9

This recording was my first venture out with White Cloud. 'An evening with' was arranged. It was a small venue and 11 people attended.

WHITE CLOUD. It is a pleasure and an honour to be here with you this evening. I thank you for your interest and your time that you have given up to listen to my words.

When I last lived on your planet Earth there was much difference from the way you live today. It saddens my soul to see the poor quality that surrounds your everyday living. When I would wake in a morning sunrise there was glory in my heart. For you, who have chosen to live at this point, there seems to be not the same surprise to a new day. There may be noise and pollution but the glory is within your soul. It is, I know, difficult for one to understand the workings of your inner souls. One is always being told to go within. Within where I hear you ask? Where does one find this inner voice? You are told, in books and such like, to be still and you will hear your inner voice. So you be still and you cannot hear your inner voice. This is something you must learn to control. Our inner voice is not actually inside your body of the flesh. One expects to ask a question and hear, as you hear in your world, a reply. Your still inner voice is with you throughout. In one instance you do not hear a long sentence of words to your reply. You have one instantaneous moment of knowing all that is needed to reply to your question. It is a knowing not a hearing. In your world you are open to hearing many things and sometimes you do not listen. You do not feel the need. Sometimes you listen with all your heart but you do not understand. When you become aware of your inner voice, there is total understanding and Love.

It is my usual fashion to speak within picture symbols that

I transmit to Blossom visually but I feel like a change. The most important message I come to give is that of Love. As you are all aware, Love is what makes your world go round. My friends, you are within a human body and you see through human eyes. If you learnt to open up your spiritual eye, you would view the panorama in a very different Light. In the same way, you have been brought up since birth with restrictions being placed upon your entire being. In a sense, you have learnt to Love only with your human heart. If you become aware of Loving with your spiritual heart you would again find it a different feeling. Again the world would look very different to you. One tends, when one is naive, to categorise Love. Love for your partner, Love for your child, Love for your friend and your parents and so on. You feel you have a different type of Love for each. You have a different type of FEELING for each, but the Love is equal. For if the Love is not Love in its fullest capacity, it is not Love.

In your world there are many lost souls. Automatically, when you are watching your electrical box, you see a picture of a particular violent incident and you condemn. If you learn to give Love to these souls who have created the violence, then that is the way to rid your world of any terrors that lie within it. Ones thought when you see a murderer, or a very darkened soul that has abused children perhaps, ones automatic thought is to say 'I'd kill him if I found him, lock him up'.... Do you not see that all negative thoughts are being sent to him on mass? As some of you may be aware, a thought when it is concentrated upon, is an energy, which becomes reality. If you want your world to be one that is a paradise in your head and your dreams, do not think of ridding your environment of these souls.

Can you imagine the effect if all on mass, that were watching in their homes, sent that darkened soul Love? Surely that would be the better option of the two.

LOVE IS THE ANSWER TO ALL THINGS.

LOVE IS THE ENERGY THAT CAN SURPASS ALL ELSE.

I understand your natural feeling towards such a person who has harmed an innocent. It is, in a sense, an automatic reaction. This is where the souls of your world have let things slip. There are souls who are in the dark. They cannot be brought to the Light by another soul that is also lost. So it is for those who have found the Light to rescue these lost souls. If you have the awareness of the Divine, then use it to your fullest. We are absorbed within human restriction. You have chosen to BE HERE NOW. Each individual soul has their individual reasons for BEING. I am not, you note, saying, BEING here! You have your reasons for BEING, but in the hubbub of your planet and the advancement of your technology you have forgotten how to BE. You know how to do, you know how to have, you know many, many things. You know the price of your vegetables in one shop compared to another. You wonder sometimes at the end of your day why you are feeling so drained. Instead of looking forward to the waking in the new dawn, your thoughts are exactly the same as they were the night before. If you took the time to just BE, then you would find... I will pause,

(At this point a lady who was late, entered.)

Welcome to you, oh late comer! I am very pleased for you to be here.

I was speaking of the importance of allowing your soul energy to BE. A time when you shut off your thoughts of what you need for sustenance the following day and how I may pay that bill? A time when you imagine you are no longer in the flesh and have no thoughts, except thoughts of Love. If you can understand, if you keep your images, feelings, emotion, on the track of Love, then your entire surroundings, thoughts, feelings, emotions, lift to another level. This does not happen overnight. It is a form of discipline. One has to learn again to think in this way.

Through greed, through selfishness your entire energy upon this planet has been knocked lower and lower. There was a time many, many years gone by, when this same ground you stand upon now, was inhabited by beings that knew only of Love. I do not feel I am telling you anything new when I say that through freedom of choice you have destroyed your enlightenment. It is now, more than ever before, that there is an uprising within your spiritual movement. More and more souls are being brought to the Light. My friends, in no way would I wish to concern you, but it is of utmost importance that the souls of your planet learn to live as ONE with all living things. When I say that, it is each one of you that can play a part in saving your Earth, I can not stress this enough. The Love that is required to save your world, is required by all. It can be done. It is important for you to help others to understand about Love.

THIS IS WHY I COME.

This is why many, many, many who are in my realm have chosen also to come to nations throughout your Earth. The message is the same from us all.

LOVE.

For those who are in the darkness of their souls, I have said this many times, it does not take many muscles to lift these sides. (*He points to his lips*) It takes a great many more to drop them. It takes one thought, as you pass by a stranger, to make those muscles smile. You do not realise the magnitudinal effect that giving that Love to that soul has. It may be that the eyes of that soul has not seen a smile for days. That soul may now go home to an empty space, sit in their chair, and they will smile. It has made all the difference to their existence. It is such a simple gesture, but its strength is a thousandfold more powerful than any movement of a muscle. The same, my friends, with your heart. It is so easy for you to brush aside ugliness of any form. If you choose to not brush it under the carpet, but instead brush up the carpet, it may look fresh and new. There is such a difference that your Love can make to a lost soul. If just one of you helps one other soul in your lifetime then you have done a worth while job. Do you not see? The soul that was able to find the Light through you, is in turn able to show the way for another and so on and so on. I feel I have expressed my point of view on that!.

Now if it is agreeable I would ask for your Love to be sent to my friend Blossom and myself so that we may have enough energy to perhaps give my opinion to a question that you may desire to ask. I would like to say, do not take my answer as ultimate - if it does not ring true within yourself, then it is not your Truth. It may be the answer as I view the situation, but in all honesty, each one of you has every answer to any question you could think about. At this stage, without sounding as a one that you call a swollen head, I feel perhaps I may have gained in the spiritual realm, a little more knowledge than I had when I lived upon your Earth. If I take a little while before I answer this is merely because I am digesting. Is there a question one of you could ask?

There is no need to be shy!

(No response)

I hope you do not mind but may I say that you are a quiet bunch! Perhaps it would assist your confidence if I said that it matters not on what form your question takes. It may be one, if you don't mind that is personal to you, or it may be of universal interest.

Yes, White Cloud, I have a question. On this Earth plane we have good health and sometimes we have ill health, especially now we have diseases like aids and cancer, even in small children. Can you tell us why this happens? What is the reason for this?

As you know, there are matters which I am able to answer briefly and matters that are very intense. I would like to offer all I can. There were and are 'bodies' in the human flesh that are pure. The soul that resided within and around this body was of pure thought. There was nothing, around, within, about the planet, that was created, that was in anyway harmful. As one progressed, which is an odd word for what one has evolved to, the choice of different aspects came, which immediately, however minute, pollutes the energy, and all that is, is energy. As time has continued on in your fashion much has been built up and disease has been caused by negative energies of all forms. You must realise here we are not speaking of one year of your time and ten people thinking not so wisely. We are speaking of many, many eons of your time. This goes into a much deeper interaction that I need to explain.

A soul may have chosen a disease in order to learn certain aspects about it's soul self. It may have chosen such deformity as sacrifice for perhaps the parents or the soul within that environment to learn more about their souls. There is choice. There is reason. If such a little soul should pass through to the other realms, it is already... booked. That time was the time necessary for that little soul either to learn what it needed to or to enable the souls that it came to, to learn what they had asked that soul to give them.

In the passing of a little one many in your world ask why, why should this happen? Especially for those in close bonding there is much pain for those left behind. Through pain one can grow. Maybe that mother or father is able to therefore open up to the All-ness. Maybe they cannot cope at all and turn further away from Love. The choice is theirs - if they choose not to, you may say that, that little soul on Earth had wasted so much energy. This is not so. That soul will have left much thought for another behind.

When the world is healed by the souls who have chosen to heal it, their entire Loving energy will have merged. This will rid your world from all disease and all pain. When one has fully learned to Love there would be no need to use pain to learn.

I realise for you, that to see another suffer leaves you with a feeling of helplessness. As I spoke earlier, whenever you feel helpless, the utmost of help you can give is your Loving thoughts. Love can remove all negativity that has formed in your matter. Does this suffice for now?

I feel that if perhaps there is a bold one among you, I could find with your help the energy connection for another question.

I am very aware that lots of young people harbour a lot of anger within themselves and abuse their bodies and minds with drugs. Do you feel that we are on self-destruct, or are young people searching for help?

We certainly are not on self-destruct unless we plan to allow such a thing if one would want it. There is a great majority of youth that feels the necessity to escape from their thoughts. As you rightly observed there is much anger. That is 'there' *(pointing to the left)*. If you look with your eyes 'here' *(pointing to the right)*, there are many young hearts that have nothing to give other than Love. They have hope and they know in their beings far more than the elderly of years in your time could ever be wise too. In actual fact, from my thoughts, the group of lost souls is nowhere near as large as the ones that are there to help us. Many in youth have to find who they are for themselves. Perhaps at that point in their life they feel that by enhancing their mind flow, they can learn, and perhaps they do. As they become wiser hopefully they will no longer require forms of chemicals and poisons to their body to find the beauty that they feel they are searching for. To each one that is angry and cross may I boldly tell you there are many more that are in the Light. It is the wish of the Divine that this is so. My friends, I realise it is hard for you to imagine a world of pure Love. Do you not see that by imagining that world you are forming a thought, which then becomes energy, which then becomes reality? That world of peace and Love is there for each one of you, if you desire it to be there. Unfortunately it will take much more than the few that are in this room. It requires what is called 'collective conscience'. As we spoke before, if we all learn to Love all, then all will become One.

I feel that I am going to leave you in rather a downward fashion. I do not desire to do so. I desire for you all to leave this room with your hearts and your souls uplifted. Although when you look around you see much sadness, it is because you have your sad glasses on. If you put your happy glasses on you will see a lot of happiness. It is merely a question of how you see something. It is your choice as to how you look upon it. Out of all things there can be good.

I would like to finish by giving thanks to each one of you for allowing me to enter into your life this night. You can not begin to understand how much this means, not just to my soul, but to many that work within my group. To know that there are places of warmth and Love and Light that we can get our message through. It is for us an overwhelming powerful Love, it raises our energies and it raises the possibilities of our hopes.

We give thanks to the Divine Oneness that is within us all. I ask that we may always remain humble and that we may always walk on the path that shines in Light and Love.

My friends, sadly it is time for me to leave now. Again my Love is with you all. I hope that I have been able to give you some hope. Remember to put your happy glasses on.

Adieu, my friends, Adieu.

CHAPTER 10

WHITE CLOUD: A warm welcome to you all.

I am showing to Blossom the image of a stream. The water is clear and pure. The pebbles underneath that lie in their place on the riverbed are white and clean. The water is able to flow freely in its purity. It is not clogged up by twigs and debris and things that have been thrown in to make it what it should not be. This is how you should imagine the flow that is running through your bodies. Disregard all that is clogging and stopping the flow. It is essential that the water be as pure and clean as you are able. Therefore the stones, being the organs that function are as clean and pure as they should be. The flow needs to circulate. If within your bodies of flesh there are masses of clutter and debris, this will stop the continual circulation that is needed to make one feel alive. The energy potential can then be used to its fullest.

I am aware that within the lifestyle of your Earth plane today, that many things may go in, but not so many come out. It is these... if I may use the word 'enemies' that remain within your flow. Your system has to cope with aliens... if you wish. Therefore all the energy that you could be using to enjoy your life is sent elsewhere to deal with the enemy, to try and rid it, to get your body back to how it should be. I am very much aware that it is not easy for a soul to always treat its body in the way it would like. I am aware of free choice. It is entirely your choice. If you were able to continue for a certain amount of time and reap the benefits, then you would think twice about going back to your old ways. You would be able to experience this life of which I am speaking.

I am giving Blossom an image of a vast mountain. At the top there is snow. Sometimes when you have within yourself a mountain to climb, because you have not been there before, it may appear that it may be rather cold and isolated at the top. It is because you have not been there that you are afraid to go. As you ascend, there will be places where you may rest and feel the warmth of the sun. You will find that when you reach the top it is not cold and frightening. At the bottom it looked as a mighty scene of snow. When you are at the top it is merely dispersed. You will find also that you are just that much nearer to the sun. In fact when you reach there it is not cold at all. It is very warming. You are able to look down and see from whence you came. The pride that arises within your soul is of such that you would not want to make the descent. You now feel safe and secure where you are. From that view you are able to look around and see many more mountains that indeed are higher than the one you sit upon. You may take time to think for a while. You may decide that you would like to climb the higher mountain now because you feel ready.

My friends, do not accept things if you are uncomfortable with them. If there are areas within your lifestyle that do not appeal, that are an intrusion to your happiness, then remove them. They will only overshadow the things that are correct. It is as if you must rid yourself of the clutter, to allow freedom to fill your days, not just for the flow inside of your body but also for the energy fields outside of your body to circulate freely. This my friends is not something that can be achieved in a matter of days, perhaps years, for all that is attached to you from your passed days will want to remain. It belongs there as far as its own energy is concerned. It is up to you to make sure that you allow this... whatever form it may be of negativity... to be released into the atmosphere. Then, when it has been set free you must allow time for the gap within your outer energy to heal. Whilst that healing is taking place, it is then that you feel at odds with yourself. I believe you call it 'out of sorts'. This is a reality that occurs. Do not feel that because you are unable to see what is going on that it is not happening. Just because you cannot see it, does not mean that it is not there. After the gap has been healed and the confusion and oddities that have been within and without you have dispersed, this is when you feel on top of the world. You feel better than you did before. Yet another part of you has come into the place that eventually shall make completion.

I am giving Blossom an image of what you call your French loaves on a kitchen counter. Some of the loaves have not been cut. Some of them are sliced, yet not completely cut through. So although they are separated from the whole, it merely takes a little squeeze from each end and once again the individuality of each slice becomes part of the whole. Where it has been cut there are crumbs that fall because it has been separated from the whole and little bits go missing. When they are pushed together, although they can feel the warmth, there are little gaps where something used to be that is no longer there. This my friends is where at times you feel lost. You are striving for that knowledge and connection to be part of the whole from where you once came. When you learn your lessons, bit by bit you fill the gap that belongs in the wholeness. I stress that they were not cut completely through.

Next to that are slices that have been severed completely. They have lost the connection with the whole. In trying to put the loaf together again, there would not be that connection that bonds them to give them assistance. They could be put together with the rest and in time with the warmth, you understand, they would adhere and once again become part of the whole or they may choose to remain apart. It is their choice never to return in this lifetime to their group. Sometimes the other slices within that loaf, when joined together are aware that part of their group soul is missing. There is nothing that can be done other than continue your life in Love. There is no point in yearning for this other slice to return to the fold. Your yearning will do little. Your Loving will do much. You must see that when a loaf of bread is created there are many ingredients that are mixed together. They are kneaded until they all become part of the same thing. They are put in the oven and the heat is turned on, as the symbolism of the Love and the life of the soul being put into the flesh, then you take out what has been created through the warmth (Love).

I would like as a bit of fun to add, that there are parts of the loaf at some ends that are crustier and harder to bite through than some of those in the middle if you understand what I am meaning!

My stepdaughter was attending this meeting. With her permission I put the following entry. I feel it may be of interest to others. She was pregnant and we had been discussing earlier matters regarding a soul entering the womb.

I am to address now a very favoured, may I be so bold as to say 'friend', who I am privileged to have with us this evening? I would like to give to you a sign of Love. I am aware that you were speaking earlier with Blossom regarding the soul of a newcomer. The interest as to whether a soul is within the embryo to start with or at birth and the different things you discussed. If you do not mind I would like to give you the knowledge that your little one is already safe within. It is able to feel your Love and has already found home. It is more than happy to remain there for the duration. It is aware already of the Love which you have to give. This is not necessarily in all cases. Each soul has different views regarding their emotions on returning to the Earth plane. There are some that are aware that they need to return for personal growth. They are also apprehensive, if you like, and they feel that they are safer in the other realms until it is finally a time when they cannot remain and their birth date is upon them. This makes no difference to the soul. This is what is correct for that soul in this lifetime. It is also, I would say, very reassuring for you that your little one feels that he is ready so early... I am afraid my tongue slipped!

It's a boy then? (Much tittering... And it was!)

She was convinced of this before the meeting and was keen to know. I do not feel White Cloud would have divulged this to her had it not been acceptable.

I should be more on my guard. To continue. He feels safe and he is eager to be with you from the beginning. This is a pleasurable thing for all concerned. It can only enhance the bonding that you shall have as mother and son. May I add that there is also a very strong connection between this child that is to come and the little sweet one that you already have. They have been very close in lifetimes many times before. They have had an agreement, if you like, that they shall help each other through different lifetimes. This is not to say that they have been brother and sister in other lifetimes. This is not so. This time they have chosen to be of this relationship. They will be very connected throughout their life's walking path.

We give thanks to the Divine Oneness for allowing this meeting to take place. We ask always that we may remain humble in order to serve and that we may continue to walk in the Light and the Love.

Adieu, my friends, Adieu.

CHAPTER 11

WHITE CLOUD: A very warm welcome to you my dearest friends.

There is always Light at the end of a tunnel unless, of course, you allow the tunnel to be blocked. There upon you are unable to walk towards the Light because you yourself have put the wall between you and this wondrous living Light. When one is walking through a long, perhaps bended tunnel, one never knows how long it is going to be before the Light comes into view. One walks blindly fumbling in the dark, walking onwards in hope, knowing that if one perseveres, eventually there will be even a faint dot of Light that one can clasp ones eyes upon. It keeps its glance transfixed in order to have focus to see one through. When that pinpoint of Light is seen it gives a tremendous surge of energy. One is able to walk with a spring in the step. As one becomes nearer and nearer, the Light becomes larger and brighter. Ones goal is never achieved with satisfaction if it is easily come by. It is through the struggle and the turmoil and the strife that you are able to find yourself and find meaning behind what you are doing. When one reaches the goal then the Light is illuminated a thousandfold, one is able to bask in the glory of what has been achieved.

It would be very silly for a soul to be half way in the tunnel, filled with fear, having not yet seen the Light, to perhaps feel it would be more sensible to turn round and go back. To go back are big errors of the heart, soul and mind. What you thought you are going back to, what once felt safe, will no longer be the same if you return. Even by walking a certain way ahead, not knowing where indeed you might end up, you have grown. You have left behind the you that belonged back there. You would no longer feel at ease because of your progression. So my friends, if you are ever feeling midway in your tunnel .... persevere .... walk on forwards .... knowing that although it appears dark at the present time, eventually through nothing but determination, that little pinpoint of Light will appear. You can move forward to the Light that you are meant to be in at that time, the Light and the place that is suitable for the upgrading of your souls. I feel I have made my point there but I would like to add something. If you can imagine a tunnel, if it is indeed a very long one, imagine that along the way there are little manholes that the lids maybe lifted to give you respite if you feel you need to rest and cannot continue. This is where you feel safe for your rest, to gather strength, ready for the continuing part of your journey. This is fine, you are merely resting, you are not receding. When you feel strong you may return to your tunnel. When the manhole lid is put back you may have the instant feeling of 'I'm back again and I do not know where I am.' Walk on a bit more, perhaps to the next manhole, take your rest, eventually, for it is natural law, you shall reach your destination.

I am presenting to Blossom an image of a goose. It is a leader. Many around are waddling behind and making a great deal of noise. It is not always best to follow a leader. Stay in silence and follow your own heart. Otherwise when the leader arrives at where it is walking that particular day, you may indeed find that you do not wish to be there. You just went along because that was what everybody else was doing. You may have thought you were following the fold in order to receive food but there would be many others there sharing and grappling for their scraps also. If you were perhaps, as one goose, to stray and go in a different direction from the others, if you venture off and be brave, all by yourself, you may indeed come upon an entire nest egg that can be eaten. You can then return to the others and invite them along to share what you have found simply by having the strength and the courage to do what was right for you.

I realise that in the way I am presenting this wisdom I have to offer, that at times it may seem elongated. I go in a very roundabout way to make such a simple point. What I would ask of you is to seriously and intently think upon the words I am offering you. As you are able to comprehend immediately what I am trying to offer, there is also, if you were to ponder deeply upon these symbolisms, a far greater meaning behind them all. What I am trying to show to you is the simplicity. If you allow yourself to keep all things simple then they do not become confused and out of proportion. At the same time, to question and query and to think and meditate upon my words, you will find, individually, different meanings in what I have to say, for each of you.

I am now showing the image of a large campfire. There are many of my kind around the exterior. We are giving thanks and paying homage to the element of fire. In our time, we had great respect for the earth, wind, fire and water. They have much to offer. Our land could not survive without these elements. I am not asking of you to become people you are not. I am asking perhaps, if you choose, to think more when the wind hits your face, to think more when the raindrops fall on your land. Think and give thanks. They are great spirits.

I would like to finish that little scenario by saying that in our time when we danced around the fire, when we danced for the rain, then by appreciating and honouring these marvels of nature, then we in turn gained much respect also.

May I indeed inquire if there is any form of questioning that would be desired to be asked?

Yes. Thank you. I was having a conversation with my mother regarding my father, who as you know has recently passed away, and wondering where he is now. We basically as humans have two ways of looking at what happens to the spirit. I know we have spoken of the spirit moving on and thinking about the lessons that he's learnt and then coming back if he needs to learn another lesson. What we live by is that once we pass on we will meet again with that particular person as we knew them when we were down here. We got a bit confused because on the one hand the spirit may have come back here as somebody else or gone elsewhere, but on the other hand we are expecting him to be there for when we pass away. So I was wondering if you could shed some Light on this?

Once again we are into a huge realm of discussion. Always, almost always for certainty, if a soul has passed on, then their Loved ones will be there to greet them and make them feel safe and perhaps show them round their new surroundings. When one has been in our realms for a certain amount of time, it is again as on Earth, one can move on in vast amounts if they choose to do so regarding their soul growth. There are stories, as you know, of souls who have passed in to our world who prefer to remain on the closest vibration to the Earth because they feel they need to be giving Love and protection to their Loved ones who remain behind. This is what they feel is a necessity for them. Until they are able to free themselves from this prospective, they do not realise that by releasing their souls from this bonding and by moving upwards they are indeed able to help and give Love to their Loved ones in a far greater form.

When a new soul arrives in our world there is a vast amount to be comprehended. If it is necessary for a soul friend to remain with that soul for a while until all is balanced. If that has been decided, that is what shall be done. You see members of your family that have passed over, no longer father, daughter, brother, or son. it is no longer of that perspective. There is a different form of family. Perhaps in respect, your father would be part of your group. This does not mean that when you and your mother are to pass to the Summerland, that you will then set up a little family unit as it was on Earth.

It maybe that whoever is meant to be with you at that time will be with you. You will not have the need for this father figure, for this is not who that soul is to you. It maybe that they have moved on a bit and you need more... I laugh at the word 'time'...to adjust, to understand where you are going. Within a soul family there will always be times when you are able to unite. It is something that is almost inexplicable because it is so different in your Earth world. In our world, if you wanted to communicate with a soul that was your father in this Earth life, you would not have to make arrangements to get a train, and what time should I go? It is merely a thought form of wanting to connect with that soul and the connection is made. This is a subject that requires many books. It is so difficult to try and explain to you what happens on the vibrations that are not of Earth. It is merely a question of thinking to yourself about what I have said and perhaps just accepting, if it feels right within your soul, or just leave it for a while until you are able to comprehend a little bit more of how it is in another realm. Many thanks to you.

I am 'up and cooking' as you would say Mr Goody. I am more than happy to perhaps answer one more question.

Nobody has a question?

We probably all have too many.

I would not want in any way for a question to be asked if the person asking felt it not the right time for them. A question should not be asked just for the sake of asking.

My friends, I would like perhaps then to take the last part of this meeting to express my extreme gratitude to you. When I saw my Blossom being born I knew that I could only be with her, unable to be heard. There were many times throughout her growing up that I felt helpless, I had to allow her to suffer pain in order for her to open up spiritually. As with many, one has to hit the bottom so you can almost be cracked open in order to allow the newness in. Disregard all that has been forced upon you as you are growing as a child. Indoctrination is a very powerful form of deceit. I waited patiently. It was not all times of despair and frustration for there were many laughs along the way. In the latter part of her life so far, I grew excited, as if indeed she was to be born again because it would also be the birth of the connection between the two of us. There is always freedom of choice. At any time I was aware that all my waiting, all my hopes could be sadly disappointed, if Blossom should so choose. As it is, through her and through souls of your kind who are willing to listen to my words, I am able to fulfil mine and Blossoms quest. It is not just a matter of sitting within this room in your fortnightly span. It is far deeper than you could know. Without you as my friends I would not have a communication link. Therefore please always know how much I Love you.

Divine Spirit, we thank you for allowing these meetings to commence and continue. In every breath that we inhale may we always remain humble and in gratitude for your wondrous force that lives in us all.

Until my friends that we should have the honour to meet up again. I now take my leave.

Adieu, my friends, Adieu.

CHAPTER 12

The following recordings took place in Australia. There were a few more meetings that took place in the last months before we left England that were not recorded. White Cloud expressed his deep Love for all those who attended the meetings, especially to Alex and Angela (they know who they are) who remained loyal participants throughout. He explained that although he would be working with me on the other side of the world, he would always be watching over them.

I began holding weekly meetings, mainly attended by people who had come for readings.

WHITE CLOUD.   A very warm welcome to you all.

Thank you all very much for taking the time to come and listen to what I might have to say. If you were able to see me you would see that I regard this as an honour and a special occasion. I have regaled myself with my headdress and my white clothing because, as I have said, it is an honour for me and for my friend Blossom to begin these meetings in the land that we have looked forward for so long to coming to.

I smile because Blossom is saying to me why have I begun with this particular image? Because I show her an image of a frying pan! I show that this pan is on what you call your cookers and that the flame has been ignited. It is then, that you put the oil in first and as it heats up it spreads around the pan. When the warmth is at the correct temperature you are able to add your ingredients. This is what I say my friends, in that you start within yourself, with your little bit of oil and you warm it up. As the warmth grows inside of your soul and the Light expands then your oil can begin to spread around your entire being and your energy field. When the temperature is correct then the ingredients that you need for your soul can be added. If, like with your frying pan, the oil is not ready when you add the ingredients, they do not cook as you had wished or at the right pace. There is a saying which I speak of many times - 'when the pupil is ready the teacher shall come'. It is with many souls that they feel they are ready to discover what it is they are needing as food for their soul. Yet they cannot find it. This is not because it is not coming to them, it is because the temperature is not quite right. It needs more time in order for this knowledge to come to their soul and be absorbed in the correct way. They become a little impatient, as you do when you are in a hurry to make your tea, you find it takes even longer because you have not had the patience to wait for it to heat properly. This is the same of which I speak about your own souls. Patience is a very hard lesson to come to terms with. When patience is running thin, then a lowness becomes part of your energy, because it is not happening how YOU want it to happen. From the depression comes the doubt and so it goes. Understand the fact that it is already there for you. All your needs and desires are there already. It is a question of accepting that you have to be within the right space within yourself in order to take these things in when they are ready to come. As you know with your cooking, the more you add and the more little things you try, the spicier and the more tasteful it becomes. You have the inspiration to try something new, once you have your basic ingredients in the pan. Sometimes you cook the same meal because that is what you do for this particular menu. Every now and then you open your cupboard and you think 'oh I will put a bit of this in'. This is what happens when your soul has become accustomed to the knowledge and the correct ingredients for you personally. Once they have settled around you, then it is for you to be inspired to try other things, to see how they mix with the recipe that was already there. Inevitably, sometimes you might add a little too much pepper and it is blowing you away! When a new thing comes to you, you want more and more straight away and then you become over loaded. It is advisable always to put a little pinch in at a time and then have a taste. In that way, as when you eat your food, it is far more agreeable to your body, not to be over loaded by putting too much on your plate, because then you feel very lethargic. Whereas if you take a little bit at a time and let it digest, when you feel hungry again you can take a little bit more until you are satisfied. This is the way for you to learn knowledge and remember about patience. If you understand, my friends, that it will come to you when you can accept it, then you will not waste time on your negative energies wanting that thing NOW. It is that it is just not correct for you NOW. It does not mean to say that the very next day might be the right time, so always use your thoughts of hope and know that these things will come. Try and let your patience be on an even keel. Like a piece of string, you know that there is something at the end, but you are not quite sure how long this piece of string is. Know that it is being drawn towards you, it is being pulled in towards you at the correct pace. Gradually these things will be yours.

I show to Blossom, flour, sugar and eggs. What you have to make a cake. When these ingredients go in and you whisk them to blend them together, they have the desired effect once you have baked it. There could be times when you have not read the packet because it is similar to another, without realising you put in to this bowl an ingredient that does not belong in a cake at all. When the cake is baked it does not mix well or rise or taste as you expected. There is something in there that does not gel and blend with the other ingredients. This is a thing that I care to speak of. For many souls circumstances arise in a souls life, and too often one allows an ingredient that does not belong to come too far in. It mixes with the other ingredients that do belong and all of a sudden your whole being, your aura, and I speak of this repeatedly because this aura is you, becomes out of balance. Once you have lost your balance it is so easy to fall. It is for you to recognise when an ingredient does not blend with the rest. This may be in the form sadly, of another soul or of a particular energy that can penetrate. When I say energy, forgive me for the misuse of words, I was not speaking of a negative energy in that sense. I was speaking of a circumstance perhaps that is around you. It is so much better to let your inner soul pick up on your immediate feeling towards this soul or circumstance. This again is not to be confused with immediate judgement because that is another matter altogether. I speak of knowing that this does not belong and blend in your cake. It is wise to deal with that immediately, knowing that it is not to be within your field. Once that has entered, it is amazing, like the frying pan if it is left too long unattended, it can flare up very quickly. This is what can happen. It is good for you to recognise these things and not allow them to enter in. It is just wise to do so!

Sometimes when one is preparing a recipe that they have not done for a while, when they go back to the book to check the ingredients they find that they have perhaps been missing out the raisins. In their head they had done it by memory for a long time, they had just forgotten the odd little thing. The cake was still beautiful. By going back to reaffirm what you think you already know, sometimes you find that extra little ingredient that makes all the difference to what you are trying to create.

Blossom is asking me now if we could get off the 'cooking' pictures!

I show to Blossom an image of a beautiful rose bush that is spread on a large scale. To look at it from a distance all you can see are the most beautiful colours that this rose can produce. The overall effect is one of beauty. If you go nearer to such a specimen you will see that along the stems, intertwined with these beautiful flowers are some very sharp thorns. It is to say that what can appear beautiful from a distance, in it's overall appearance, is not necessarily what lies underneath. It is far better to look at an ordinary bush of your weeds. It does not look very appealing but when you go closer, when you bother to go deeper, you can see that weeds can produce the most beautiful little flowers from their buds. This is a fact my friends.

When I speak of judgement, it is not for you to look at another and ask yourself why perhaps you could not have the same attributes on the outside of you. It is not for you to look at yet another soul and feel sad because of their outer portrayal. Perhaps you may say 'Well at least I have this and at least my whatever isn't as bad as this'. All these things that people tend to judge from the outside.

I feel it is important for you to learn to strip away the flesh of all souls that come into your path. Look inside of them. Imagine them as their colours. The colours of their aura are who they truly are. As many of you are already aware, in the realms in which I reside, this is how we recognise another soul, by the brightness of their colours and the different colours that they have. If we see a soul whose colours are dim, then we know that we can offer our Love and our help. I have spoken before that it is good for you to imagine your 'dimmer switch' that you have for your electrical light. If you feel that a soul has dimness, sadness and loss around their energies, then just visualise turning up their dimmer switch. Visualisation is a very powerful energy. It will only take you one, two, three seconds to brighten the energy field around that soul and it will have an effect.

I show to Blossom now and she has absolutely no idea where this one is going! - one of your little monkeys. It is swinging from branch to branch and tree to tree in massive leaps and bounds. It does not think before it leaves one branch to go to the next as to whether or not it can make that leap. It has the inner trust within itself to know that it can swing. It will catch hold of the next branch, then it can let go and catch hold of the next one. It trusts what it knows. If the monkey was to stop in a tree and look across to a tree that was perhaps of the palm variety and the main trunk does not have outlets for it to grasp onto, it might ponder and doubt as to if it took that leap would it be able to cling on and grasp around the trunk? The minute it begins to wonder, the minute the doubts come in. The more the doubts come in, the more the fear comes in. Once the fear comes in, the thought of even trying to do it at all seems to be a big concept to this little animal. This is what happens with you on this Earth at this time. It is wise my friends, to think out a certain matter. One must look at where one is wanting to go and indeed, what will be there for you after you have taken this leap. If your soul feels right about doing so, then trust this. Inevitably if it feels right within you when you leap, you will without doubt catch on to the trunk. The minute you start wavering regarding the pros and the cons, different energies enter you and you might never make the leap at all but swing back to the trees that you feel familiar with.

Trusting is a major issue as we are all aware. Trusting what is out there and trusting what is within you - it is the same trust. What is out there is part of you. If you learn to trust yourself and have the confidence and the belief in yourself, you will find that not only can you leap and grab the trunk of the palm tree, but in doing so, many coconuts may fall at your feet as an added bonus! You have followed your truth. So many people are afraid of doing this simple thing. They go against their truth and they wonder why they are feeling so out of sorts. Sometimes my friends, it is good to stop. Instead of looking where you have always looked and all that you are familiar with, look somewhere else perhaps or a little further ahead. If that looks appealing to you have the courage to make that leap. Once you are there you will find that you can see many other types of trees that you did not know even existed beyond your familiarity.

I am aware that because of my excitement I have what you might say, babbled on and I have disregarded that perhaps you may like to ask a question of me that I may be able to advise you upon. If it is agreeable with you all then we will see how we can do on the scale of our energy vibration for Blossom and I. If it becomes that I must take my leave then sadly we must cut it a little short. I have no preference to what type of question you may care to ask. I would fully like to stress that my reply is not a direct yes or no because that is not my position. If I can give some advice on that subject I would be happy to do so. So I will keep quiet for a moment.

The question that was asked was of a personal nature regarding a soul that had passed to the 'other side'. A reading had been given to the lady that asked the question in which the soul who had passed was able to talk with White Cloud and then White Cloud passed the pictures on to me to be relayed. What was given was passed on to the family concerned. It gave them hope and strength as nobody knew of the matters that were dealt with other than the personal family. Therefore I would care to mention the answer that White Cloud gives here as again it maybe beneficial to others.

Is xxxx all right? I was wondering how he felt after coming through in the reading?

Straight away I give to Blossom the image of this man, with such a humour it tickles me, running around a football pitch with the trophy in his hand. Blossom can even hear the music for what they have on the television for the football program. He shows within the nets, footballs stacked to the brim within the goal. For him, dear lady, this is what he felt he had achieved. He could not have dreamt, because of what he thought before compared to what he knows now, that what he was able to convey and the fact that it could be relayed to the souls that needed this message, it has made, as I say, his goal full of footballs. He shows himself lying flat out on the football ground. He is laughing but exhausted. He is very content because he knows that this is not the end, it is not a cut off for him. He was concerned of this originally. He is saying that he understands. He knows it is not possible to come to every football match if you like. When he knows that there is a game where there is a seat for him, then he feels at peace to know that when it is correct for all concerned, that he may again send Love and hope to his family. Thank you.

It is, if I may say, that he is laughing with you. He does not want you to be sad, he is touched that you have tears, but he does not want sadness from you. He wants you to be happy because he is this way. It is pointless to be sad because this is not his intention.

Are there any other questions that one may like to inquire of? Perhaps you like me speaking too much!!
My friends if it is agreeable we shall bring this meeting to a close. I would like to thank you again for your time that you have given to listen to my words. I only hope that I may be able to pass on the wisdom that I have gained, and in time, to fill you with all the knowledge that I have from the place that I reside in now. I would no way presume to underestimate your own intelligence, thoughts and emotions. I feel that what I have learnt is valuable and therefore it is my desire to share this with as many that are willing to listen.

We give thanks to the Divine Oneness for allowing this meeting to take place. We ask always that we may remain humble in order to serve and that we may always walk in the Light and the Love.

My friends I now must take my leave. If it is possible I ask you to think on these words and to take the truth for yourself. If it does not feel agreeable to you, what I say, then by all means reject it.

Until we have the pleasure of speaking again I send you all my greatest Love, my hopes and my strength, until next time,

Adieu, my friends, Adieu.

CHAPTER 13

WHITE CLOUD. A very warm welcome to you all.

Blossom is smiling because I am giving to her the image of what you were speaking of earlier. I am showing to her the image of a washing line.

A few giggles due to the fact we had been speaking of the mundane chores such as washing etc.

It has on it many clothes with the pegs keeping them on the line. I show two lines, one of which cannot be seen because it is packed full with the drying of the clothes and one behind this, which is empty. Now, it is strange that when the washing was hung up, it all had to be put on the same line next to each other, instead of having space in between each article and using also the facility that was behind it. Sometimes it is that the soul packs in everything so tightly within their everyday living and it leaves no room in between. It would be beneficial if one did one thing and then add a space in between before rushing off to do the next. By having this space it allows your energies to re-balance and for one to become aligned within the self. You may say that you do not have the time to do this in between each job that you have to perfect that day. I am not asking for one of your half-hours, I am merely suggesting perhaps five of your minutes. This would make such a difference to how you went about performing your next task.

If you took the five minutes to take some deep breaths, connect with the Oneness and generally re-balance, then, when you go to pick up the keys to your automobile, it is with a different attitude than it would have been without giving yourself that five minutes. You will find that when you are driving you can appreciate what you can see, instead of looking directly ahead and feeling very tense with everything that you are doing. When you have finished that task, then again if you have to go somewhere in your car from where you are, sit in your car and just re-align. You will be surprised, well in actual fact you will not be surprised at all - it makes sense, the difference this will make everyday. You will find at the end of your day, when you are just going into your evening, that you have so much more energy to enjoy your relaxation time. It is not that it MUST be done. If you could just attempt this, when you feel you can slot it in, then because of the benefits, you will find that you choose to do this more and more. It would also be greatly appreciated by your soul if you were also to do this upon waking. Not to lie on your bed when it is time to awaken and spend five minutes that way for you will return to your dream state. Rise and perhaps move around for five or ten minutes and then sit somewhere. Take five minutes only - that is all that is required to greet your new day, for your soul to greet the beauty that lies ahead in your next twenty-four hours, for it to connect to all that is there, ready to come to you. Most importantly, remember to give gratitude for what is to come to you that day, to thank in advance. Then you are giving appreciation to the universe knowing that there is much that is to come to you. It is different if you say, in a bit of a whirl in your mind, 'please, please, please let today be a little easier than it was yesterday'. That is almost as if you are on your knees begging for forgiveness and mercy. THERE IS NOTHING TO FORGIVE. So it is better for the connection to KNOW that things will be and ARE better today than they were yesterday. As each day progresses in this manner there would be no need at all to have the thought of, 'please make it better', because each day would be so fine.

I am now to go back to speaking of the empty washing line behind the full one. It is a question of looking around to see what is available to you in order to benefit and gain the ultimate performance from what there is. Your clothes would also dry far quicker by using the line behind as well, because they have so much more space to be individual and blow freely without being squashed and compressed by another. Because of the routine that one has allowed to be the custom of your day, it is sometimes, that you immediately do what is to be done. You sometimes forget to look around to see if there is another way of doing it that could make it simpler for you.

It is sometimes, as with the line behind, that you just shut your eyes. It is as if your eyes are blinkered because the manner in which one has led so many days of your life path has become set. It is so refreshing to the soul to take all the washing down, throw it into the basket and for a change, walk around and find branches that you can hang your socks on, or a fence that you can dry your towel over. To change the way you do your routine things can uplift your energies immensely. Not only that, it is giving you far more pleasure to look around and think, 'where could I hang this to help it to dry?' It is a challenge you see. It is through challenges that the energies can keep circulating. What happens with these every day routines can be done blindfolded. It is repeated so often that no Love is put into this duty. Everything in your energy is then becoming stagnant because there is no excitement, there is no exhilaration. So with these things, perhaps it is more fun to do them in a different manner. As you are aware my friends, to 'do' anything of any nature, the same as to 'speak' of anything of any nature, if it is not done with Love then it should not be done at all. It is not good for your soul because it gains nothing for you in your growth. When you are washing up or doing your ironing put some Love into what it is you are doing. Look at that item of clothing and give thanks that you have nice things. If you appreciate and give thanks for what you have then it is reciprocated by the atmosphere. That is the only way to put it. Giving thanks and giving Love are two of the most valuable assets that one can possess. You would be amazed, and this time I mean you would be!, if you could tap into energies that you cannot see with the human eye. If you were to see what effect Love and gratitude has even in empty spaces you would surely be 'bowled over', as you would say! Those energies spread and spread and connect and magnify and attract. It reaches to where there are none. When those thanks and Love reach to places of darker than Light, it sparks off a little flame and with the winds of change the flame becomes brighter and a new Light is created for souls that have been in darkness for a long time.

I am showing now to Blossom the image of your 'Snow White'. This is how you should go about your…I do not like to use the word 'duties'… but if you appreciate what you have in your home and give thanks and Love, then it should be a blessing and you should sing as you go around keeping it clean. You are appreciating and giving thanks. All that you have you need to keep nice and be proud of, however little or however large these articles in your home are, however new, however old. If you find there is something within your home that you do not enjoy polishing, then discard it, remove it from your home. Those energies do not attract you, so release it and leave the space there for something to come in that, you get a duster every day to shine and see. It is that the Golden Rays will emanate from this new thing, in turn that will make the inner energies of your house shine also.

It is beneficial also, and please I do not mean to tell Grandmothers how to suck eggs, that to play music in your house is a wonderful experience for the energies that dwell there. It matters not whether it is of a melancholy or a vibrant nature. It is the sounds that can connect with these energies. It is exactly the same as what you know as your Feng Shui. Have the windows open and let the air circulate. All these things make Love in your house. Because of the Loving energies that are in your house, it also then reflects upon the nature of your relationships that dwell within. There is cleanliness and pride and Love and Light. It is very difficult for two people to get angry quickly with each other because it is highly alive with Love. If you allow slovenliness and do not appreciate what ever it is that you have in your possession at this time, then the energies fall low and therefore it is much easier to pick up on those lower energies and feel lower within yourself.

This is what I am saying my friends, when you are sweeping your floors and you see the dust, know that the dust is negativity. That has to be, because you must have opposites. Know that you are removing that negativity and releasing it outside of your home, that must thrive on Love.

As an after thought because every soul has with them Angels to protect them, perhaps bare in mind that your Angels also have to live within your home. Therefore it is nice for them to help in their work, if it can be done within a pure environment. It is for them a vibrational thing. If they need to be close to you at certain points to help you along, they might have to move all this fogginess which makes it more difficult for them to connect with you.

This is also what I am speaking of within your auras and your energies. If you keep raising your vibrations in Love, in Light and in gratitude, how beautiful your colours are, how much they keep moving. They keep circulating and growing and because they keep moving, you can move freely. They can connect with you far easier. Do not allow the darkness to penetrate. Visualise when you have your little five minutes to see if you can pick up on how your aura is today. Ask 'how are you today?' With practice you will see. You will perhaps see that somewhere around is a little blockage, a darker patch that is restricting you in someway so visualise in anyway you desire, for instance I show to Blossom getting a spade and digging it out, so that the gap can be filled and you may continue. Whichever way, dust it, remove it. Whichever way you want to, visualise it for yourself. You will learn to see these blockages within and remove them so that this can continually keep you alive. You will find also by doing this that ailments that are bothering you, be they large or small, will disappear. These darker patches in your aura are also connected with physical things that just need to be sorted out.

I feel, if it is possible, that there is time and energy for us to answer a question if there is one that is desired to be asked.

I wonder if you could tell us about soul extension?

This is a tricky one because Blossom has no idea what you are speaking of!

I am showing to Blossom the image of a red flower. This flower is deeply red, the circle in the centre is black. This is not to do with darkness of any kind. I show that this flower is as it should be - perfect in every way. In the narrow flowerbed there are seeds that are planted all the way along. Some of them have already begun to shoot and some have not. The knowledge that they are under the earth as seeds planted and rooted is known by this centre flower. There is no doubt that they are not there, because they are all the same variety and therefore the connection is just 'known' as to their whereabouts. I show that if the wind and rains were to come and knock over and deplete the energies of this main centre flower the seeds could not even see what is happening, but purely because of the connection of the seeds that are along this path, they are able to pick up what has happened. They are connected so strongly. By sheer thought energy these tiny little seeds, by amalgamating thought, would be able to send those energies along the row to reach the root of the flower. They would be able to give the energy, strength and life required for this main flower to once again stand in all its glory. Now, that does make sense to Blossom, but she is interested to know if it is in anyway connected to your question?

Yes.

That is marvellous. Blossom is saying 'Phew!'

My friends. I am very pleased that these meetings have begun. There is so much that can be discussed and as Mr. Goody is not with us today, I am very honoured to sit amongst the women all by myself!

My friends, it is time now to take my leave. I have enjoyed this coffee morning immensely.

We give thanks to the Divine Oneness for allowing this meeting to take place. We ask always that we may remain humble in order to serve, and that we may continue to walk in the Light and the Love.

Adieu, my friends, Adieu.

CHAPTER 14

WHITE CLOUD: Good evening to you my lady friends. It is again a pleasure for me to be in your company.

I am giving to Blossom an image of the time in which Jesus Christ was crucified upon the cross. I show on the hillside the image of His Earth Mother and also of another lady, of the same name. I show to you that also at that time when this major event took place that the 'heavens' as you sometimes call your sky, were opened and the rains fell down. It was as if the whole world was crying because of the sadness that had befallen mankind.

I show that because of the sorrow within the heart of these women that were so connected to this high spirit, that where the rain fell, as they looked to the ground, flowers immediately came up.

Blossom is asking to clarify as to whether this was a reality or whether I am talking in terms of symbolism because of where this is leading? You can perhaps work this out for yourselves as I continue.

Their eyes, in sorrow, looked to the ground and I show that where the tears from the world fell, immediately a little flower that is white appears. It is as if, although the atmosphere was so oppressive at this time, where these little flowers came up, because of their purity in the colour of white, these little places had their own Light and they gave a little Light around these special souls. I am trying to say to you, my friends of the feminine variety! that because of the strength that lies within each of you, when it is even the moment of absolute despair for you, through your tears you are able still to find the strength and courage to see rays of Light amongst all the darkness. Not only that, it is that your thoughts can make them grow in the places where Light is least expected.

I show now that many, many, many years later, when the existence of that time was erased from that place, if one was to look with their spiritual eye, they would find that the entire field is covered in these little flowers. It is like many things my friends, one soul could go there and they could use their spiritual eyes and being and they would in turn shed their own tears for the beauty they beheld. Another soul could stand in exactly the same place, but that soul, for reasons that only itself can deal with, has decided not to open that spiritual eye. It shut it off many, many, many moons ago and has not yet had the courage to open it to see what it may see, so it stands in the spot and all it sees is barren land. For this soul it does nothing. Perhaps in turn the tears are shed by that soul because its heart is empty and can see nothing.

My friends, every day, when going about your business think if you can of putting Love into your chores! Think also, when you are outside in nature, of beginning to be aware of this spiritual eye, even if you do not yet know how to use it. Begin to practice using it although nothing is happening at the moment. I realise that this does not quite make sense. It is like with anything that you begin to develop, if it was to be a musical instrument, like your piano, at first when you look at the notes on the page and you look at the notes on this beautiful instrument - what that little dot with a line actually has to do with these bits of wood, who can say? How could the two ever be connected to make such music? By perseverance and by learning, understanding, connecting, patience, then bit by bit a sound is produced. When you come back again for another practice, a little bit more can be played without discord, until an entire symphony can be created out of these ten digits *(shows hands)* - that are connected to this, *(points to arms)* - that are connected to this *(points to head)* - that is connected to this *(points to eyes)* - that are connected to the notes on the page. It takes many, many, many hours to perfect an entire symphony. So when you are beginning to use your spirituality, because that is what you are in essence, it is not something that is completely estranged to you - it is what you are. So it is remembering this, recalling what you used to know and developing all that has been shut away for many eons.

So if you were to be, as I know many of you do, sitting on the headlands, what more beauty could you ask for in your country? When you look at the colours of the trees, contrasting with the blues of the sky, in harmony with the blues of the sea, what more could you hope for to exhilarate your soul? It is then that you ask to recall what you truly are. That is all you need to do for lesson one! Then you work on that each day and by your next lesson, you may find that lesson two perhaps will give you something new to work on. My friends, I could not give you lesson two as a steadfast rule. Like with all music teachers, they all have different ways of teaching and they use different information in their exercise books. So it would be that on lesson two, you would look out at the sea and become aware and still yourself and wait for your teacher to arrive. You would find that perhaps each one of you has the same fundamentals but the way of bringing forth your music is different to each. It is also that Blossom can be very aware of this from her past, that when you have achieved a piece of music then you cannot leave it alone. It is that you have two minutes to spare so you pop to your piano and play it once more. You feel such joy from your achievement. It can be played through, here and there are little errors, but in general you work upon that particular place, so that there is no longer a barrier in your mind. You will find my friends that the more you practice this awareness the more the desire to try it on something else. You do not have to be at this headland. You can be anywhere, inside or out. You just learn to tune in to the spiritual side of what is occurring at that moment in this space of your life.

I am showing now to Blossom an image of what you call a toffee apple. This is, shall we say short but sweet! in that, my friends, on the inside is the goodness, the part that gives you nourishment. But oh so often is the goodness enclosed by an outer shell that really is of no benefit at all. It will not leave you lying on the floor very sick, but in turn it will not either, when absorbed, do you much good. It is that in your lives, if you come across a shell that is not good, remove it. Remove it with Love, but remove it. It is then that the goodness that is inside can be seen by all. Why would one want to clog such a beautiful fruit with such weight? So many souls do not realise that they walk around blindly, encompassed by the caramel. You see my friends, if you would allow the suns rays to come onto the caramel it would become sticky and melt away. I can not stress how valuable it is to your souls, if you give time and visualise the warmth and that Light from your sun pouring into your heart and into your solar plexus and into your chakras. It is the essence. It is your food for your spiritual soul.

So too my friends, the moon. Imagine when you are of an evening looking in amazement to the stars. It is that the Light of the moon is also entering your spiritual self. If you can imagine that the pull of the moon can move an ocean backward and forward, imagine what strength it can give you if you allow it to come into your very being. In that way you have invited the masculine and the feminine, the night and day, the Light and dark, you have asked all things to come into you. They can balance themselves to give you perfect harmony.

I am showing to Blossom now, and we are swapping and changing rather a lot!, a picture of a pram that was used in the olden days. It had very large wheels and was made of very thick metal. It had an enormous hood and a very large handle. All in all it was rather cumbersome. Look at how this invention has progressed. Instead of having to open your door and manoeuver this monstrosity of a contraption - that bangs the paint on your door and takes up so much time and energy and with such a minute baby inside! - now you pick the baby up, you flick something with your leg and the whole thing is all of a sudden this big *(shows size)*. You can pop it on your shelf. So much has changed for the convenience of every day life. It is because at a point a soul came up with the inspiration of taking a weight off a mother when they were out walking. They came up with the original design of a large pram. Once that was set in motion and materialised then the inspiration for other souls came quite easily, to change its shape and size it down to make it as it is today, which is far more amicable.

So it is my friends, that within yourself as an individual, utilise what you are presented with from an internal and external point of use. It is for each soul to be inspired as to how to make the most of what one has and the most convenient way to use it. What is right for one is not necessarily right for another. I do not know of this country but I know that in England there were ladies that chose to push these very large prams. That was their choice, it obviously suited them. It maybe that you look at another soul and see that they are doing something completely differently from the way you would choose to do it. Indeed assess the situation to see if you can pick up some hints or prefer to do it that way. If this does not sit well with you, do not doubt your own capability of doing it the way that came instinctively to you. The minute you put doubts into anything, because you feel that somebody else is doing it differently and you ask yourself 'are they correct and you not so?' then your whole being becomes unbalanced. Believe in yourself! For all you know that other soul is looking at you feeling exactly the same thing! Go by your feelings. If by what you are doing and feeling and expressing feels right within you, continue to follow. If it does not feel right, look around for ways to adjust until the feeling, the expression, the doing, does feel at one with yourself.

My friends, it is, if it is agreeable with you, time for our questions. Is there a question that may be asked?

I have a strong pull towards the Hawaiian culture. I wondered if I should follow this through?

(Although this question is of a personal nature, I feel the answer can be beneficial to others)

My friend, it is what I have just spoken of. If it feels right then go with it. If it does not, allow their souls to follow their paths and you walk another. If you indeed are even attracted to it then there must be a reason for this. If when a soul is attracted to something and they get there, it is very rare that they are disappointed, otherwise they would not feel the magnetic pull in the first place. It could be, as with many things of this nature, that in another lifetime you were highly connected with the ways of these people. It could be also that what your soul needs at this time is to connect with the ways of these people, because they can give you what you need. That is why they are calling you as they do. They know by your soul giving out the need. They have heard your call and through the winds they are bringing you to them. It matters not the reason for your attraction and connection. The result is what is important. Thank you.

If it is all right we may speak a little more or have another question because I do not like it to always be what I wish to say. I am more than happy to speak of something that interests you particularly

We are now being taught that many of us here are what we call 'star seeds'. Do you have an opinion on this?

It is not that I have an opinion, it is that I have a vast amount of knowledge!

My friends, again by all pleasure, I would be happy to speak on this with you from the start of one of these gatherings. By all means let me know when you desire to learn or recall of these matters. I have a volume of things that I wish to speak of knowing that the company that we are keeping is in acceptance.

My friends, as I'm sure you are aware. A soul's evolution can only be where it has evolved to at that point. As we have spoken of, in the spirit realms, a soul cannot be on a plane in other realms that it is not in tune with and has not yet evolved to be in. It simply could not take the higher vibration. It has been known many times for a soul to take a glimpse because it would prefer to be there, but it could not reside in that space until itself has grown in Love and learning and knowledge. Then, and only then, when the Light and the vibration are correct may it glide into that level. It is the same here with souls who are completely unaware that there is even a continuum of their souls after what you call death.

So to speak of planets and life, that a soul that is sitting here may possibly be from, really would not be a wise decision at this time. With a soul that has not advanced in any way, remember this - by putting Love into thought you could find a little opening that might just get them thinking and spark that flame that lies dormant within. There is a way for all souls to get on their path home. Its just that many souls feel safer in the picnic area!

My friends it is time on our energy level that again I must leave. It is enlightening for myself and Blossom to be working in such a strength together and so regularly. I offer you my thanks, because if you were not desiring to hear my words, who would we speak to?

We give thanks to the Divine Oneness for allowing this meeting to take place. We ask always that we may remain humble in order to serve and that we may continue to walk in the Light and the Love.

Adieu, my friends. Adieu.

CHAPTER 15

It came about that I was asked to do a couple of days reading in Brisbane, the beginnings of 'my travels' with White Cloud. I was pleased to be able to accomplish four in a day. It was rather daunting as I was not sure if the amount of energy required would be there to deal with this many. I was thrilled to know it was. We had a very enjoyable time, leading on to more visits.

WHITE CLOUD. Welcome to you my dear friends. It is comforting to be amongst familiar faces after our little journey away.

Again I bring forth the image of the man that was known as Jesus. I am showing of the time when the lashes were placed upon His back. My friends, within each of us, are deep wounds that are now healed over. It is, depending upon how deep these wounds penetrated into ones self, that the regeneration of that place of flesh and bone is of a different quality from the rest. Simply, it was damaged and by being repaired it is then different from what it was before, because it has been replaced. This is why one can see sometimes upon the flesh a discolouring of the skin because it is not the same as the rest. It is as if that scar is always there to remind you of how it got there. It is my friends, with wounds to your heart and to your very soul, that by the sheer depth that is created with pain, that when one is slowly recovering and the scars are healing, that it also leaves within you and within your auras discolouration from the colours that are your true self. With the flesh, when one is young the wounds can be healed far more quickly. Little ones when their senses are hurt are very quick to continue their play and not allow such types of hurt to cause them pain. In many cases they can heal quickly as with their flesh. As one grows with age and wisdom, one becomes further removed from their spiritual home, they allow the pressures of the Earth plane to sink upon their shoulders. They allow sometimes the wounds to become deeper than necessary. It is as if they are taking a knife and digging it deeper in order for them to acknowledge how much pain they are really in. My friends, it is far easier when you have this pain of heart, soul or mind, not to continue to dig away at it, but to immediately go to your medicine cabinet and take some balm and plasters and give it the treatment it requires to make it better, not to make it worse.

I realise that sometimes the pain is so continuous and nagging that it does tend to drag you down. It requires acceptance, first of all to accept this pain and to acknowledge where and why it has come to you, then to decide that you have had enough of it. Once you have made that decision, then that is when you go to your medicine cabinet and you change the way that you feel. You do not allow this to impose upon your self and your energy field any longer. It is that you must be adamant that you will not allow this to continue. Sometimes my friends, it is that another soul has so much pain within them that they need to off load some of it onto another. If another is going to accept it, then they will continue to off load their pain. If one decides that they shall not allow another's pain into their energy field then it can be stopped, purely and as simply as that. Put a barrier and protect yourself from energies such as I have been speaking. Then what will take place is that when this soul desires to give you their pain it will simply bounce itself off your protective barrier. It will come, sadly, back to that soul a thousand fold because the force of your barrier is so strong that it will rebound and give them more pain. It is then that the change must come, because you can no longer take their pain, then you must against all odds give them your Love. Do not rejoice in their quantity of pain. Do not say to yourself, 'you get what you deserve'- they have not found Light my friends as you have. Send them the Light so they can feel it and they can see it. You will find then that they will take their pain and off load it into an empty space where the winds can take it far away to be dispersed. They will be left in a void and they will not know what it is that they should fill this void with. They have been so enwrapped in their own ugliness. If you, if it be only you, that sends Love, then that seed can be placed in that empty space. If you continue to water that seed then it shall grow into a beautiful flower and it will encompass that entire space that was once empty. It will be that because of your thoughtfulness towards another that as the rose garden inside of them overflows, they may with their own permission, pick you a bunch of roses from inside of their heart, for you to display in your house of Love.

When I first began, Blossom thought this was a bit of heaviness to start with, she was correct but it needed to be said. I change to show to you the image of a child in a playground and I show a slide. If you note when a little one is climbing up the steps of a slide the parent or the guardian is very aware that this child may fall to the ground. The child is so occupied with the pleasure that it is about to undertake that it has no fear. It is the guardian that has the fear because it has seen what can happen many times before. When one feels that they are at the top of the ladder, fear of what they have known comes upon them and they do not allow the pleasure to stay. Instead of being at the top of the slide and looking around at the view from the top, they are already thinking that in a minute they will be at the bottom again! They are expecting this to happen. It is as if they say to themselves 'Well I know this can not last' and automatically you are sending those thoughts out so that it shall not last. If you look at a child on a slide it goes to the bottom again screaming with glee. It reaches the bottom at great speed and automatically it wants to go back and start all over again. It is not affected when it comes to the ground.

My friends, please do not feel that I am flippant in the way that I speak of this because I am very much aware that, that of which I speak is far deeper than the little game I am giving to you. What I try to explain is, sometimes one can feel so on top of the world and then just like that, they feel that everything has gone. They are at the bottom of the slide so quickly and they did not even have time to enjoy the way down. Be like a child. Do not feel as if you have gone so quickly and landed on your behind and sit there and cry. Get up, without staying there to feel your pain, get up and walk round. Dry your tears as you go. Do not dry your tears sitting on your behind, get up first and start again. As you get to the steps, indeed you may feel 'But what if I fall off again', there will always be lessons to learn, but this time, go again with determination. When you are getting to the top why not take a rest half way and look around because when you get to the top you are very soon at the bottom! Look around step by step as you go. It may be when you get there, there may be another that is looking rather afraid of the journey down. It may be because of your experience that you can go together. Because you have already been there you can put on the braver face. You can hold that other soul as they go. Because you have been there so quickly before, this time you learn to just keep your feet a little apart to stop it going so quickly. You go slower. Although it is exhilarating, you learn that by doing so, when you get to the bottom it is not going to be such a crash. You can get there and step off. You want to do it again. You want to be at the top at least when you hit the bottom it is not so disastrous.

There is a saying in your world that everything is very much swings and roundabouts. When one is on a swing, it starts off building momentum. Quite a lot of work is involved regarding the leg muscles in order for the swing to become higher. With many things my friends, it seems that the hardest effort must go in at the beginning in order to get things swinging. As one gets higher it can then take its own rhythm and one can feel the excitement of the wind as they are reaching higher points. It is then that when one stops working their legs that the swing begins to slow down. Eventually it comes to a place where one feels comfortable with the height they are at. It can sometimes make the insides rather queasy because of this movement, so one needs to find the correct rhythm in order to remove this. Sometimes the queasiness does not disappear until the swing has completely stopped and they have got off and walked away. As the soul gets off the swing because they feel queasy, instead of sitting on the grass to get back in balance, they immediately go over to the roundabout. This is still and, as this soul gets on it, it goes round and round and gets faster and faster. Again this feeling of queasiness is brought up inside until the point where the head goes round and everything is spinning and one feels terribly out of sorts. When eventually it stops, which takes far too long, the soul gets off and can hardly walk in a straight line, everything has been shaken up inside. It sits on the grass and feels dreadful! My friends, sometimes one may put a lot of effort into something that they feel would make them high, only to find that when they reach this point it is not as enjoyable as they thought. Then sadly, they have to wait until it comes all the way down again. Even then they do not appear to learn their lesson, immediately they go and try something else, waiting for that 'buzz', believing that they need that 'buzz'. You would have thought that common sense, when they got off the swing, would make them just sit and be still on the grass for a time. but no! - because so many souls feel that if they are not living life to the fullest then they are not living at all. This is not the case my friends as you know. It could be that when one first arrived at the playground that the sun was shining and the sky was blue. They chose to simply lay down on the grass and give thanks for the beauty they can see with their eyes. They had no desire to go on the swings and the roundabouts. They know that what would make them feel the highest of all is to lie and be at one with all that can be perceived.

I show now in the playground you have what is called a climbing frame. Sometimes it is that you watch a child become almost ape-like in the way that they can swing from bar to bar and hang upside down and do all manner of things. Again your fear is always guarding them, telling them to be careful. Do you not see they have no fear? Their fear comes from you telling them to be careful or they will fall. You are placing upon them the fact that they will.

I realise, my dear friends, that because of the Love in your heart for these little souls, that your desire is only to take care of them, because it would be painful for you also to see them hurt. With all manner of words, little souls can become fearful timid little mice. Simply because we are adults who, of course, know best!, we tell them that if you do such and such, then such and such will happen to you. It is as if we literally have a garage full of bricks and mortar. Slowly, slowly, we build around these little ones a huge brick wall. It would be far better that instead of bricks and mortar that we had straw. Then, were they to fall they would have a much softer landing. Should they decide for themselves that actually what that adult told them might not necessarily be their truth, then it is far easier to blow away the straw as opposed to taking a hammer and knocking down this massive thick brick wall.

Would it be fine now to have a question because that might become one that needs more time to be spoken upon?

Can you please tell us a little bit more about 'star seeds'?

Perhaps it is that we cannot go into full detail of this. What I show to Blossom now is the image of beautiful twinkling stars in the deepest night sky. It is if you were to imagine, when a child has a piece of paper with many stickers on, of all different sizes of stars, they put the big star first, and coming from it are the little ones that come down. I am showing that where there is the main star of your sky and indeed there are far more than the eye can perceive, there are little droplets of stars, many of them, that keep coming, keep coming down to the Earth plane. One would feel that this at some point would stop. I am showing to Blossom that it is a continual feed through of these little droplets of stars that come. A certain amount of them land in the same spot. There is a little crevice that is placed upon Earth for them. It takes a certain amount of them, and as they become settled in the Earth's atmosphere, they gel together, before they place themselves out of the crevice as one. These star seeds, as you call them, unite and continue to appear as the one star. This I realise has not clarified much, it is a little food for thought. It is quite complicated in itself to even try to give a simple explanation. Trying to put it in to simplistic terms can become quite complex in itself!

I am showing to Blossom some graph paper. Upon this graph are certain peaks. There are rises and falls. I show it starts off and becomes a little bigger and a little bigger until in the centre it has reached the peak and then it makes its way down again. If this paper was to be never ending then I show that once it has come down it would begin to build up to the peak and down again. This would be in perfect rhythm and harmony. It would be as if for a certain time along the paper that the outcome was a replica of the others. Further down the line the pattern begins to change dramatically. So too, this would stay for a long, long piece of the graph paper, then again it would change. This, my friends, is what is taking place upon the Earth plane and in other galaxies. This is what is taking place inside of you. So when the pattern suddenly changes, of course you are going to feel a bit strange because you are so used to the way it was. Suddenly it is different. Then when you have got used to the difference and have settled in nicely with that, you continue along and then WHOOP BANG off you go again. This is part of the course my friends. When you feel that 'Whoops!, here we go again!' - look forward to it. It is change, it is not boring, it is change and it is exciting. You do not know if you are going to go down or up or across. Just go with the flow and enjoy the ride.

My friends it is quite important, more so than you are aware, for you to do your meditation and for you to have this time with me. Please understand I do not mean from a point of view of myself, but purely by the knowledge that you are gaining, that is already in you. Because of the energies through the meditation, through to this *(placing hand on heart)* you are bringing much more to the top than simply the words that you are hearing from myself or should I say Blossom.

It is beginning, my friends, and I am very happy to go with the flow.

We give thanks to the Divine Oneness for allowing these special meetings and times together to take place. We ask that we may always remain humble in order to serve and that we may continue to walk in the Light and the Love.

Go in peace my friends until we have the pleasure of speaking again.

I leave you for some reason looking at the graph, with that very familiar song on your Earth of 'Climb every mountain'. When one reaches the top there is such a view to be seen.

Adieu, my friends, Adieu.

CHAPTER 16

WHITE CLOUD: A warm welcome to you all. It is nice to know that I am becoming so renowned!

This comment was due to the number of people that were attending the meeting that evening.

I am showing to Blossom an image of what a musician would have upon their piano. It is a box that marks time in order for the musician to play in time naturally. There is a long rod and upon it is placed a square of metal that I imagine to be a weight. If this weight is at the top of the rod, then it is, if I have done my calculations correctly, that the timing is very slow from one side to the other. It is perhaps that the music that would come from something of this timing would become rather melancholy and perhaps even saddening to the soul. It is as if the weight is bringing down your whole energies. Also the heaviness of the music brings down the energies that are around you, as if there is a brick either side of your shoulders weighing you down. My friends, gradually, if one was to move the little square a little further down, then the rhythm quickens a little and the music that is played becomes a little lighter. So also your energies pick up a little as well and they brighten in their colour. When one is awakening every morning and in their souls and their hearts there is no Love and there is no Light and there is no purpose, then it is as if for them that their very day is heavy upon their footsteps. The only music they can hear in their soul is that of morbid sadness. It is that they walk with their eyes pointed to the ground because they are too in darkness to look around at all the beauty there is to purvey.

My friends, as one learns to walk into the Light and their soul is moved up just the tiniest bit from this heavy weight, then again when they wake up in the morning, their tune is also Lighter and so is their step. They no longer look directly down but perhaps just a little way ahead. As they realise that what is a little way ahead is actually a little bit more interesting than looking at their shoes then they have a desire to develop this. It has sparked off an interest. It is so that when one has accustomed themselves to the particular rhythm and they feel in tune with this, the entire vibration around the Earth is lifted higher into the Light and into the Love. It is that when one wakens in the morning then the brightness is 'let me get up and get out to live this day', it is with a spring in their step. They no longer look a little way ahead, they can look straightforward, they have a focus, they have direction. The music they can hear is so exhilarating and enlightening to their very soul. They have moved further up into the Light. The further ones soul moves into this Love the further ones soul expands to take up more of it. Sometimes I am aware that it is as if the little square box is right at the bottom of the rod and that the music is so fast and the dancing is a swirl inside of you. Then, all of a sudden, it is like somebody puts the lid on, shuts it up and it has gone. It has suddenly stopped and you wonder what has happened. This, my friends, is when you must take note of where you are at. For a while things must come to a standstill in order for you to align your soul with the place that you have come to. When the lid has been put on and it is quiet and it is dark, these are the times when you look inside yourself in your silence and you look at where you are. You give thanks for your blessings. When this has engulfed your senses once again you are ready to dance your dance. Your batteries have been recharged. When the lid is removed, in order to be in control, it maybe wise just to move the little square box down yourself, just a peg or two, so that you can gradually bring yourself back into the swing of things and do so at your own pace. Sometimes it may seem to you that around you there could be many metronomes, or simply just one other. It seems as if this metronome has completely different timing from you. It is as if the noise that is 'tick, tick, tick,' that is different from you, puts you out of balance. So you try to get along the same as the other, this cannot be, because it is for each individual to go at their own pace. To live in their own Truth not that of another's. If one tried to catch up or slow down with the sound of another then it would only confuse. It would be that the mechanics would eventually give way because it was not living the way that particular metronome was designed to.

So it is my friends, never be perturbed by another's pace. Do not try and fall in line, HEAR the sound of your own heartbeat, FEEL the rhythm of your own heartbeat, LISTEN to the rhythm of your own heartbeat. It is when you start to listen that after a time you can hear another metronome that is placed in exactly the same place on their rod as you. It can be that it is just one or many metronomes, but you are in harmony together. You are in balance and rhythm together because you have stopped to listen.

It is fascinating my friends because I am aware that one is told or guided to listen to ones inner self. One would think 'But I cannot hear a voice in here. My ears hear the outer sounds'. Listening to your soul is more of a FEELING that you can hear, if I may put it that way. It is when somebody says to you 'Your answers come from within'. You sit there and sit there and nobody is saying anything inside. It is, do you understand the reality of the emotion. This is where your answers lie. It is not that another 'little you' will pop out and say 'I know the answer to that one at last.'

You see my friends you are laughing, but so many are waiting to hear that voice! When they do not, they become frustrated and even walk away from this inner guidance that is their Truth. That is, if I may be so bold, their God. When somebody says to you that God is within you, that is what they mean. It is YOU. It is your FEELING, your LOVE. These are the answers that are within you. Take the time and the patience to sit every day just for five minutes to still yourself. Be patient. Any quandaries that you have of any kind, ask for your inner self to guide you. Then, my friends, let it go, be in the stillness of the nothingness. When I say the nothingness, it is in fact, the All. Let it be that your mind stops, your heart slows. Become in tune with the nothingness that is All. You will find that, perhaps when that day you have stopped, or perhaps taking a nice walk, that out of nowhere that answer comes to you. It is because you have allowed it to be brought up from inside of you and come to the surface where it can be heard.

It is not a... I desire to use the word 'ridiculous' thing to do, you know my friends, to just sit and switch yourself off. You would be astounded at what just five minutes of turning yourself off can do for your soul, for your entire being. You could take five minutes of your day wondering what you should do next. Choose to sit for five minutes and allow the energy that 'is' to surround your energy and to blend with your energy. You will find that as you progress each day, by doing so, when your eyes do awaken in the dawn of the new sun, it will be as if your metronome has been oiled. It keeps it's own rhythm without any effort. It is a quickening for your soul if you take these five minutes a day.

I am showing to Blossom now an image of a pillow that is crammed full of tiny feathers. I show there is a pillow fight. The feathers are consuming the entire room. These tiny little feathers when separate from another and as individuals, are such soft light beautiful little things. When they are on mass, inside the pillow and cannot be seen, one would never know that this pillow, this solid mass that one rested their head upon had so many beautiful things inside. It is that when a fight takes place and the feathers are thrown all around, they can get in your throat, they can stick together. They cause chaos over the entire room once they are let loose. I am showing to Blossom that a soul is with this empty pillowcase and it is an arduous task to pick these feathers up and put them back inside the pillow. When all have been picked up and put inside, the pillow perhaps does not seem as full as it did before. It is lumpy. Everything has been completely rearranged. It is as if it is a completely different pillow but, when one goes to lay its head upon it, it may just be that because of the difference of the feathers inside, that it is actually more comfortable. Before it was not quite where you wanted the puffiness to be etc. So it can be my friends, that sometimes when you have what you feel is your security, what you know is your place to rest your head, when it is all scattered into many different places, it is as if everything that you knew as secure has been literally blown apart. When it comes back to you again, when you retrieve what is worth retrieving, when you take the time and patience to collect it all together again because it is precious to your soul, when you have put it back into your pillow, it is actually far more comfortable than it was before. It was necessary for the change.

If you will excuse, in that Blossom does not feel that I have been very explicit regarding this. In order to keep the energies flowing we will leave it as it is, but I would like to be bold and say that I am a little wiser than Blossom and that I know that the message has reached those that needed to hear what I was trying to say! I am wondering if it is agreeable, because we have such a wonderful gathering this evening, if it would be all right with all that are here, if we may have a few questions now, if it would suit everybody?

A *long pause*

I have to say I am amazed! because I would think that sometimes in your week there would be many questions that you

would think 'I will ask White Cloud about that at the next meeting'- then when it comes to this nobody has anything to say!
Laughter throughout

Would it be preferable for me to continue if nobody has a particular question? or would it be that I should keep my mouth shut a little longer until somebody has one?

A lady attending the meeting that evening had been to a private reading with White Cloud the day before. We thought perhaps the batteries may have gone on my tape recorder as the reading did not come out as it should have done when she listened to it later.

When the batteries went flat on the tape yesterday, was that meant to be for me to think this through?

My friend, in my Truth I would say to you that although one can listen to my words on your little machines and feel that they are triggering off new thoughts from the last time they listened, in all Truth when my words are spoken to you soul to soul, then it is taken in straight away. You feel that you had not grasped all that I had said because perhaps you were thinking or you were aware that you could sort it out later, but everything my friend that I said to you has gone into your being. It is a question of allowing to hear it inside. It is, I would say, that it was not by Divine intervention that I played with those batteries. This was not so. I am sad if you feel it was necessary and you do not have those words. I am sad if you feel that way my friend. It need not necessarily be this way, you heard my words and what was needed was absorbed. Whether one would agree with me or not. You are fully aware of the answer to my question. I do not in any form appear to be of flippant words with you my friend if it is coming across to you that way. What I mean is that the answer is in here *(hand on heart)* anyway. What I say to a soul in a private confrontation - that is not a good word I feel - it is merely that when I pick up on your energies, I am explaining to you what is around you anyway and what is very accessible to you, without me. Sometimes, for certain souls, I am able to read these energies in order to help a soul move a little further down their pathway.

Is there another question or shall I continue for a short while longer?

There were no other questions.

I am showing to Blossom an image of a set of knitting needles with some knitting that has been created upon them. The wool is of a pink colour and it is as if the stitches are magically being knitted. I show no hands. The needles are automatically doing their work. I show that these needles continue on and on. When they come to the end of a row they turn round and they start again. As one is aware when this particular art is performed, then the growth of that creation becomes visible. I show that this particular piece of knitting becomes longer and longer, so in the end the bottom of it is folded up, it needs to be kept neat and tidy. I would say to you my friends that if you are spending a lot of your time and putting a lot of work into something make sure that you have room for it to be seen. What is the point of working on something so creative and from yourself? It is not bought from a shop, it is by your hands that you have created this article. Do not let it be folded up and out of sight so that nobody can see it. I show that if one is to do this knitting then it should be that the end should be tied around a lamp post and down to the next lamp post and all the way down the street so that the bright colours can be seen by everybody who walks past.

Each one of you my friends has inside of them so much talent of all forms. Do not waste what is inside of you, because each one of you, different and individual as you are, is aware of what it is that is burning inside needing to come out. Some of you already are displaying these beautiful gifts. Others think that 'Oh one day I might get round to doing this' or 'I've always liked doing such and such but other people seem better than me and it always made me feel insecure'. Whatever it is inside of you, my friends, that is nagging away and never goes away as the years pass, do yourself a favour and open the door so that it can come out. Do not hide your Light under a bushel. You may look at another's talent and feel that what they do is so much more magnificent than this little thing that you desire to do. What you do not realise is that this little thing that you can create, that other soul that you looked at is probably looking at you to say 'Oh I wish I could do that!' Do not compare yourself with another. It is like with the metronome, do not fall into another's pace my friends. Bring out your own rhythm and your own music. Please I ask you, if you listen, whatever gifts are yours, bring them out for others to see. It is not that you are showing off. You must understand that by showing a gift to the world you are in turn giving so much to another soul. They are able to receive from you. When one receives then, in turn they can give also and so the circle goes round and round.

I show before it is time to leave, a large bush. In the centre, underneath amongst all the leaves there is a little light bulb. There are only little specks of Light that can be seen through this bush, unless you put your hands in the middle and you spread it so that the Light can come up through the very centre. Do you understand? Through the centre of yourself. That is your Love. Let then the Light be shown to all around. It is your right to shine my friends. It is your given right. Do not hide in the darkness - it is so much warmer in the sunshine.

May I say that I am very proud that I have been able to speak to new souls that perhaps may not cross my path. I am very honoured that you have taken the time to come and listen to a very old man. I hope that wherever you wander across this planet that you will remember my words about the Light. If you never lose sight of the Light then your world will always be smooth to walk upon. Whatever trips you desire to take will always be a beautiful experience.

We give thanks to the Divine Oneness for allowing this meeting to take place. We ask always that we may remain humble in order to serve and that we may continue to walk in the Light and the Love. Take care my friends until we may have the pleasure of speaking again.

Adieu, my friends, Adieu.

CHAPTER 17

WHITE CLOUD: A very warm welcome to you my friends.

I am showing to Blossom an image of a musical toy. It is a very small piano that a little toddler would enjoy hearing the noise of. Blossom can hear the tone of this little toy and compared to a grand piano it is not very pleasing to the ear. My friends, to the little child that is playing, it matters not whether the sound comes from the toy or the matured instrument. It is merely the noise and the different notes that are appealing to their ears. It is because their ears at that stage have not yet developed or become attuned to the fine - tuning - excuse my English! - it would be that because of the resonance that takes place inside the eardrums that it would just be the difference in pitch that the little one could differentiate between. It is only as the child grows and the workings of the ear develop and become more attuned that they are able to hear the difference between a beautiful piano and a toy one.

It is, my friends, that you can, now you are more developed in your spiritual being, become attuned to a vibration that is, if you like, appealing to your senses. It would be that if the little toy piano were played you could not listen to it for very long because it aggravates. In the same way as you have become aware over your time that you cannot stay in the company of certain souls because it aggravates. Their tune is not as refined as yours is now. It is a necessity to blend in an orchestra with each other so that the tunes that are played make beautiful harmonies together and therefore the overall sound is of intense beauty.

Do not concern yourself regarding what I would call snobbery. This is not so. It is merely that you cannot tolerate for your ears, for your senses, to be too long with that sound. You have practised and as you practice you have brought to yourself fine instruments to play upon. It is so, that now you are able to be in your orchestra, that the music you are able to play together can be heard by souls that are also attuned to receiving such music. It would be that the souls who have not accomplished their tasks, would prefer to attend a different concert because that is where they are at home. This is agreeable to all. It is not your concern. Let it be that perhaps in your open-air concert your music maybe carried by the wind across to the other concert. It maybe that certain souls can pick up a finer tune than the one that is, if you excuse my slang, that is 'in your face.' Their ears can hear this calling from further away. It is that all of a sudden the resonance and the discord between that soul and that music can be no longer bearable so that soul may wander off. It is that for a time that soul will be neither at one concert or the other. It maybe, my friends, that they choose to sit in a field of solitude and compose their own music until they can find what sounds 'pretty' to them. Once this resonance has surrounded that soul, then it can be drawn to a higher level. When it has found its Truth and its own level, which is higher from the concert it was attending, it takes time to adjust. It is sometimes that you desire to be in solitude in order for you to know where it is you are.

It is sometimes more disconcerting to join an orchestra that you are not quite up to standard with. Then, when the music is placed in front of you, you cannot play as well as the others. This brings doubt and confusion into your being. It is far better to be by yourself and work on your own at a piece of music until you feel you can play this piece blindfolded. When you have accomplished and perfected your tune, then you can have the confidence to go and play it with the others.

It is also as I have spoken before regarding the metronome syndrome! - the conductor may be conducting with his baton at a pace that is a little too fast for the level YOU are performing. Therefore it is important, imperative to go at your own pace. I know that I have spoken of this for many weeks. My friends, when you are learning a new way of doing a mathematical problem you do not just do the one exercise and it is deeply implanted, you have many exercises to complete before you are assured that it has sunk in and it will always be part of your knowledge. This is why I feel it necessary to repeat what one can work with, in different analogies. In that way you cannot become bored of what I am trying to say to you. You must not feel inferior if your level and your knowledge at this point, to your view, is not as advanced as another. Inferiority does not enter this world that we speak of because we are all equal.

My friends, know that the Light you have around you is the same Light that is around another. It is from the same source. It contains the same knowledge, the same Love, the same power. It is simply a matter of finding out more information about it that can brighten it up, if you like. When I say this, I do not mean in any way that because one may have more knowledge than another, that, that is why the Light is brighter. NO! What one feels in their heart is what makes the Light bright. How one puts into action what is in their very soul to another, is what makes your Light brighter. Whether or not you are aware of greater things, does it matter? You still wake up every morning and clean your teeth and go to the shops and continue LIVING your life. But if one is aware of greater things it raises the consciousness. It is helpful to wake up to this because one day it must be done. As to when you decide to open the curtains and look 'out there' is your decision only. As I say, if you choose not to open the curtains for another century or so that is your choice. Nobody can condemn you for this. It is your pathway not another's. It is just that sometimes, my friends, a soul can peep through the curtains and shut it again because it looks so bright and so beautiful and so alive that they feel that would be too much for them. So they hide behind the curtains. Sometimes a soul may need to draw them back a bit at a time. So they can adjust, whereas other souls decide that they ARE ready. They pull them open and there it is and there they are! They are ready to do it that way. Understand that for others it is too much to contend with, too much to comprehend. It frightens them. They are not used to such beauty, as a reality. It is not in their feelings to know that they deserve such beauty and this is why they cannot take the Light. This is why my friends you must practice and rehearse your orchestra as much as you can so that those people that do not even like music can hear your song. You can bring them out into the Light.

There is, if Blossom can recall, a question that she wanted to ask. She was dusting a photograph of a lady who was the great grandmother of her son. This lady was not spiritually aware. She found life to be very miserable at times and it was always 'Why me? Why me?' She has now moved to another vibration. Blossom was thinking that when a soul who is unaware passes through the mist, a different understanding takes over this soul. What she wanted to know was, if that is the case, why do they come back again? Is it that they have not learnt what they were meant to open up to that time around? If suddenly when they move through they know it all, why would they need to come back?

I am showing to Blossom a shawl that has been crocheted. There has been much time and effort and Love that has been put into this creation. It can keep a soul protected and warm. It is a delicate, intricate merging of material. By a simple movement of a stick, a finger and lace, a beautiful pattern like a snowflake miracle can be created. As one puts more time and effort into this, so it grows. At some point, for the soul that is crocheting, it feels the article is complete. So it gently finishes and ties off and there before them is their creation. Somewhere, within that work, there may be a time when that soul was watching your 'box' and the concentration was not a hundred per cent. A little stitch or two or ten was dropped, it was missed by the eye. Then, my friends, when it is finished, by not giving all the care that is required, gradually the little stitches that were dropped become bigger and they expand into the rest of the work. I show it is in the centre of the shawl. Gradually this makes larger holes in this beautiful shawl. If one can rescue these stitches before it is too late, then there is little work to be done to reinforce and again make it complete. Making sure, this time, to finish off very tightly. But if one sees this and it is a case of 'One day I must get around to mending that' - again one knows your saying 'A stitch in time saves nine' - the longer you leave something to be repaired, the longer time it shall take to repair.

Blossom has no idea if that has answered her question or not! But I know that it has and for her to listen to the tape will confirm this.

Again, before I take my leave my friends, I would like to reiterate how very grateful I am to you for giving me your time. It means a great deal to me, for this I am truly honoured and blessed. Also Blossom and I would look pretty funny doing this to nobody!

My friends, I ask only for you to contemplate my words. In your own ways, turn my words into actions. There are many souls that I myself am aware need Light and Love, but however hard I try they cannot hear, feel or see my Love. They can hear, see and feel yours. If, as we have said before, we can turn one soul who is tone deaf into a musician then we have achieved much.

We give thanks to the Divine Oneness for allowing this meeting to take place. We ask always that we may remain humble in order to serve and that we may continue to walk in the Light and the Love.

I am aware my friends that these meetings are taking a holiday. This is a time for us all to take a break and have some fun. As Blossom knows sometimes we can take this all a little too seriously. Jump around in the sand. Splash in that beautiful ocean you have out there. Enjoy what you have at your feet. Again my friends, Happy Holidays to you.

Adieu, my friends, Adieu.

CHAPTER 18

WHITE CLOUD: A very warm welcome to you my friends.

I am showing to Blossom an image of a large book. It is opened in the centre, on either side there is writing. There is writing throughout all the pages. I show that the book is upside down. It is then that one side is flicked over, so that there are many more pages on one side than the other. If one tries to read something that is upside down it makes the strain on the eyes and the mind far more complicated than necessary. Sometimes people choose to continue because they happen to be in that place and prefer to struggle a little further in order to find out what they want to know. It would be far easier to make the effort to stand up and walk round so that the page is agreeable to your mind's eye and if that indeed was too much effort you could merely get hold of the book and turn it round. It is looking at something from the correct perspective. It may seem that when the book was upside down, that the side you were trying to read had only a little bit left. When you turn it round you realise that you have many, many pages to get through. It is far simpler if you allow yourself to take the agreeable angle as to what suits you. Then you find it is very easy to read and each page can be flicked over very quickly because it is compatible to where you are at that time. I show also that one is tearing out the pages of this very large book. They are being crumpled up and put into a bin. This is not all the pages, but some. It is that many things can come in to your perspective, into your circumstance, and immediately you know that you do not need them. They do not agree with the rest of your story. So it is necessary to get rid of them straight away and put them in the bin because you do not need them in your life.

I show now to Blossom an image of a Golden Sword. The rays that emanate from this sword light up all that is around as if it is the aura of this sword. It is, my friends, that we have chosen to fight the Good Fight. For those who are on Earth at this time and have chosen to work in the Light, it is that a long, long time ago there were many, many who volunteered to do this work on Earth at this time when it was required most. It was your choice. You volunteered and you were chosen. You were each given a Golden Sword for your strength. When one is feeling weak and feels sometimes that they can fight no more, it is then that you must hold your Golden Sword to the skies. The rays from the sun will energize the Sword once more. The energy will travel through the Sword into your hands, through your hands and into the soul and into your very being. Then once again you are renewed with strength. There is no battle to be fought. There is merely the necessity to hold your sword in front of you and let others see its Light. They then can put down their old sword that is rusted, heavy and battered. The minute they put it down their hands long to be put round the Golden Sword so that their cuts and their wounds can immediately be healed by The Golden Light. It is for you my friends, to march on. When your legs are weary then you must rest. When you have regained your strength continue to march on because there are so many souls that are hiding behind trees, behind walls. They have already lain down their swords but no Light has come to find them. There are many, many, many souls who await your assistance. It is said also that souls that require the Light shall be brought to you. In many cases this is so. In many cases many souls are afraid of the dark. They are afraid to move from where they have fallen. Therefore it is up to you, if you choose, to march on and look around the corners of the trees, look in the darker places where sometimes your eyes do not find it appealing to enter. Know always my friends that your Golden Sword is your protector. It is your Light and your strength. The minute the hand of a soul in darkness can hold on to the strength of the Light of the sword, then their souls immediately are released of the burden of the darkness. You may lead them into the path where once again they may see the blue sky shining down upon them.

There are many groups like us who are honoured to have Higher Angels to be with us and give their Love. When I say an honour it is the only word I can find in the vocabulary that comes anywhere near close to what I wish to describe. When one goes about ones daily duties, sometimes we, as you call it 'tune in' and other times we get on with our business. It is for you to understand, that always there are Angels, guides and helpers at your side. They are there to give you anything that you desire. It is good to talk with them. It is good to send your Love to them. For them it is a bit like walking along and nobody is paying any attention to them, as if they are being ignored. But of course they are wiser than this, the joy that fills their hearts when they are acknowledged is a Light that illumines the world.

So now I would like to ask if there is a question that anybody would like to throw at me?

It is interesting that you mentioned about guides. It is something that I've never thought about before, that I may have my own personal guides.

Do you desire me to speak of this?

If that is all right?

Guides are drawn to a soul through the connection of Love. They do not necessarily belong to the family that have been on Earth, either from an ancestral point of view or nearer the lifetime that you are living. This is not the case, your guides can be so, but usually your guides are drawn to you through the connection of like minds. Guides are of a higher plane than sometimes family maybe at this time. Helpers can be of the family unit or they can be made up of any soul. If a soul that is living on Earth requires help, concerning a particular aspect, then it is not necessarily that the helper has been jogging along with them all the time, waiting for that moment to jump in with their little twopence worth. It is that the connection through Love can immediately bring them to you when it is required. It is perhaps that your guide can ask for them to come. The guide can seek out a particular soul that is required to deal with that particular matter and can offer advice. It is in general that a guide stays with you. It is also accepted that if a soul does not desire for the guide to be known to them, in most cases, even then the guide will stay. Sometimes it is that another guide may take over because that new guide would be able to connect with the soul that chose a different pathway. It is sometimes necessary for another guide to deal with this, because they are more suitable than the guide originally chosen. It is not in any sense a failure. It is just progression and how a soul decides to walk his path and what change maybe necessary.

My friends, due to energy conditions taking place today, it is that we must cut this meeting a little short.

We give thanks to the Divine Oneness for allowing this meeting to take place. We ask always that we may remain humble in order to serve and that we may continue to walk in the Light and the Love.

Adieu, my friends, Adieu.

CHAPTER 19

WHITE CLOUD: A very good evening to you all.

I am showing to Blossom an image of a cutting board and upon it is a long vegetable that you call a leek. There is a large chopping knife. The knife is chopping the vegetable into many slices. I show that the vegetables are put into a pan of boiling water. After a time because of the heat, the vegetables that were once hard become soft. It is that then they can gel into the wholeness again. Sometimes, my friends, what appears in a soul to be on the outside to another soul, what you would assume to be a hard case, is not always what is on the inside. If you were to give that hard case warmth then gradually that warmth will soften the hard case. It is, for some, that their lives have been chopped up into many pieces. For some souls it is easier for them than another to put the pieces back together. For other souls, it is for them that they have been sliced so many times, inside of them has been cut and wounded, therefore they build this shell around them so that they cannot possibly be hurt any more. They may come across to you as a soul that has no feelings, this does not mean that you should walk away. It is as if inside of them is calling to have this shell broken down, but they are too afraid. If you were, my friends, to take the time to give your Love to these souls and it would require much time, much patience and much understanding, then gradually you would see, as if there was a crack made in the shell, a little bit of what is inside is able to be released. The more you feed the crack with the warmth and the Love, the more then the space can be opened, until eventually, as with a nut in its shell, when the crack is big enough it can be broken and discarded to reveal what is inside.

I show to Blossom now, an image of a Lady of Mercy, that is dressed all in white. Next to her I show a Sister of Mercy that is ordained in black. It is that they both give with their hearts in the work that they do. They do the same job, but one looks totally different from the other.

I show now, for your amusement, that the nun in the black and the nun in the white are placed upon the chessboard. You have your players in black on the one side and in white on the other. When one is playing this game on the board it is a question of thinking about each move that one makes in order to achieve the goal that one is setting out to do. Sometimes one can see immediately the correct move that would be of advantage to that soul and it is a move that requires little thought and also a move that can go many steps forward. Other times one has to wait and survey the whole game in order to use tactics to move in a way that might not seem at first that it is heading in the right direction. This is confusing for Blossom because she does not know how to play this game. Coming the other way, you may find sometimes that where you think you would like to go is blocked because there is an opponent in your way. It may be that by one move from the other side, everything that you had planned has gone out of your window. It would mean that you have to view the whole situation all over again and consider a different way around in order to achieve your goal. Also, an opponent can remove your team, your support, your back up can suddenly be taken away. You find that what you thought was solid behind you is no longer there, but you still have to continue to finish the game. When one is playing this game one uses careful planning and one sometimes has to take risks. You do not know whether the risks will be beneficial always, but sometimes you can see no other way to move your players. Sometimes by taking the risks you may find that you are knocked out, but you still have other players that you can use. Other times you will find that it was worth taking the risk, because it brought you forward and you find that you have come a long way by taking that risk. Luckily the opponent had not seen the cleverness of your move and you are there... solid. You will find also that as you are getting nearer to your goal, then things that are in the way, because it is at the end and you have come so far, will automatically be removed for you, in order for you just to step in and know that you have come all this way and you have reached your goal. As I have explained other times in different aspects, sometimes when you see where you need to be it does not always happen as smoothly as you would like. You cannot just jump from square to square in a straight line to get there. It is sometimes that you have to work hard and contemplate. Sometimes though, you need to have rest, you have to go different ways, a longer route, it is a planned one and it is the route you have to take. Each way along the path you stop to think. You pick up and you learn many aspects of the changes around you. Ultimately if you believe that you can get to the other side of the board then nothing can stop you.

I show now that there are two of your dice being thrown. When this takes place, unless of course it is a dodgy dice, one has no idea when it is thrown what numbers these little boxes are going to land on and what is the number facing on the top. One always, more often than not, would desire that the two numbers on the top are double so that they are the highest numbers of six and six. This does not happen often. Sometimes one dice will have the six and it finishes rolling before the other. Your heart and your mind is willing it to be another six. Sometimes it could be a two or a three of the lower numbers and your heart sinks. It is that sometimes in one's path way it seems that a particular thing is going exceedingly well for you and it makes you happy and strong and very confident. Also positive because it is six, it is six on this one particular thing. At the same time it may be that there is another circumstance in your life that is only a one or a two. However many times you throw this dice it does not go higher. The balance tends to weigh you down. Instead of concentrating on the six, concentrating on the one that is going well and using all thoughts towards that, one tends to keep throwing the two and that is what they are wasting their energy on. It is better sometimes to leave something that is not going your way when you have tried and tried, to just put it aside and concentrate on the things that are going well. Maybe it is that the timing in all things is not ready for you with this other dice and if you leave it aside and concentrate on something else it can no longer pull you down and you can no longer be wasting energy on something that is not quite ready for you yet. Then, when you have used everything to your full capacity with these other things that are zooming ahead, at one point you will suddenly remember that 'Oh a long time ago, where did I put that dice? I remember that I put it aside because it was not working for me' You find this dice and because it is the right time, you throw and it is a six. It makes you think and so you throw again and again and again. It might not always be a six. It might be a four, five, six, but it is definitely looking better than it was before. When you have the confidence that the six shall always come, then you can pick up the other dice and you throw them together and you find the two sixes come. They are ready now to work together and compliment each other.

I now show because we seem to be on a theme of games, that there is a board of what you call snakes and ladders. This is very much, my friends, how life seems to be when one is growing within the soul. Sometimes you come to a square when it is your turn and the ladder takes you a long way up. It was so easy to get there. Then you go along for a while and suddenly for no reason at all within side of you, you come to a snake. You fall down half way from how far you have climbed. It is a disappointment because you felt you were getting so far. You have no option other than to continue your game. You may come along so far and then come to another snake. You seem to be always losing your drive and your power. However hard you try you seem to be coming further down. Again you are in the game of life. You continue on that game. You may come to a ladder that only moves you up a little way, but at least it gave you a boost. It gave you the determination. It lightened your energy. You had been getting very fed up when you could see that others were ahead of you. You continue and you come to another ladder. This time it is a bit longer. So the game continues. It takes perseverance to reach the end. For me I would say that in the game of life there is not one loser. Everybody can reach the end of the game. My friends there are many, many games if you would like to call them this, on your pathway through life.

Are there now any questions? I enjoy so much being able to let somebody else speak!

Yes, I have a question White Cloud. There is a soul who we are aware of that is struggling to keep mind and body together. Is there any practical way that we can help her, other than sending her loving thoughts?

The lady in question had tried to take her life the evening before.

My friend, as I assume that all that are gathered here are aware, that by giving thoughts to that soul, and her family also who are very much in need, this is a very effective and powerful way to lighten not only the energies on the outside, but the heart that is broken on the inside. Also, as you said, there is a practical advantage in that this lady, whom I have also spoken with, is suffering from loneliness and so obviously the more she knows she has people who care, the stronger she will become. Also my friend, there is an aspect that this soul is on her pathway. As with all souls there is freedom of choice. There are many souls in this world and in other worlds who have lost all meaning to themselves. There are many workers who choose to offer their Love and their help to these souls. It is a decision of the lost soul as to whether they choose to come back into the Light that is offered or whether they are content for this time to stay where they are. I realise I use the word 'content', but in some cases their soul does not desire to move on. There are different reasons regarding their energy that has been with them since they began. Never, my friend, give up hope on sending Love to such souls. One can often, sadly, be disappointed. This is not of your concern. It is a fact that one can only offer all that one has, one knows when it is time to stop and to move onto another, because sometimes that soul is not ready. One does not understand always how it is that a soul here is able to pull themselves out of the mire. It is that they have more strength to struggle and pull themselves out, even when they can still feel that they are being dragged under. Although at times they feel they have no strength left they do not give up the fight. They can see the land and if they can get to that they know that they can grasp on to something and they can get out. Whereas another soul does not have as much physical or mental strength because they have not built it up. It is that sometimes they reach a point where they do not care whether they are dragged under or whether they reach the shore. They have lost all survival instincts. They feel that if they were to go to the next world then their struggle here would be over. This is not the case, but that is for another evening when we have more time. By all means continue to rescue this lady, send her healing thoughts always, because as you know, those thoughts are energies that can be reached. They will touch her and they can, if she is willing, lift her. She knows from her reading the choice she has and the goodness that can come from her life if she finds the strength to do so. Thank you.

Is there another question? So you know all the answers do you? This is fine for I feel it is time to take my leave because of the energy link that is beginning to become very thin.

My friends I once again would like to thank you for giving up your time to listen to the knowledge that I have gained throughout my path. It is an honour for me to have ears that are willing to listen. Where there are ears to listen then there shall always be my voice.

We give thanks to the Divine Oneness for allowing this meeting to take place. We ask always that we may remain humble in order to serve and that we may walk always in the Light and the Love.

I hope my friends that I have given you some incidents to ponder upon. Until we have the pleasure of gathering together once again, please know that my Love is with you. Many thanks to you once again.

Adieu, my friends, Adieu.

CHAPTER 20

WHITE CLOUD: A very warm welcome to you all.

Although this meeting we are small in number, that does not mean to say that we cannot create a lot of power and energy.

I am showing to Blossom an image of the sea shore. After the sea comes the sand and after the sand comes many, many pebbles. When one looks upon this view, one can see that not one pebble is the same. Because they are together on mass, they become as if they are the same. It is not until one sits down and is gently playing with the pebbles, that without thinking they look into their hands, they look at the different colours and shapes that happens to be within the one pebble that is in their grasp. The more one looks, the more one can see how fascinating this one piece of stone is. Then one looks at another pebble and it is picked up. You look deeper into this and you see that it has completely different facets from the other, though just as intriguing. So it is my friends, that it is so easy for a soul to walk down the street and it passes many other souls. You may happen to notice a particular item of clothing that is attractive to you, but in general you walk along going about your business. It is for you, my friends, to take another soul as if it were a pebble on the beach. If you were just to take the time to look into that soul and find all the beautiful intrigue that is individual to that one soul, then how differently you would look upon it compared to your original view.

I show now that a pebble is being picked up and is thrown into the water. Some people are able to play the game where a stone can be skimmed many times across the water leaving a ripple with each touch of the water, until it drops down. Some people do not have that knack because it involves a flick of the wrist - the pebble falls into the sea and immediately drops to the bottom. It becomes frustrating because they see another that can go on maybe seven or eight times. It is that some souls are able to acquire a talent for certain things without any trouble at all. It seems to come naturally to them. To another, this same talent requires much practice and even after much practice and determination, they still do not have that flick of the wrist, and they become doubtful of themselves. This should not be so, it maybe that the soul who cannot grasp the knack of throwing the stone, could then turn round and kneel in the sand and create, with the hands, the most beautiful piece of art out of a million tiny grains of sand. It maybe that the soul who can throw the stone many times to flick in the water turns to look at this and feels that they would like to do this. They kneel in the sand, but however much effort and concentration they put into making their creation with these minute grains, it would be an impossibility for them to create something as beautiful as the other soul who has a talent for that. It is, my friends, important for you to realise that we are all individuals. When you see another being able to do something so well send them Love, be grateful that they have been given a talent that can make you feel beautiful by looking at it. Do not make it appear to you that you are insignificant because you are unable to do what another can do. Every soul has many talents that are inside of them that are awaiting to be brought out to give joy to others. If one is not aware of what their talents are then it is merely a question of being patient and asking to be shown. There is not one soul that does not possess these gifts.

I show now a little toy sailing boat that is bobbing along on the edge of the sea. I show that the front of it is too heavy and it continually puts its nose down. Gradually, as the water fills the little toy boat, it will go down and sink to the bottom. When it is retrieved it is again put on the water. The same thing, time after time continues to happen. It would be wiser, when the little boat has sunk for the second time to the bottom, instead of continually trying again, to take the boat out and look at it's design. By studying where the balance is going awry then one is able perhaps to put a couple of pebbles into the back of the little boat so that it is not top heavy. When again it is placed in the water then it can bob along without any problem at all. It is a question of viewing the situation. If one side is weighing you down too much, then it is so easy if you look into the problem to correct it. All it took was a couple of pebbles. Often so much time is wasted by continually putting the boat on the water and hoping that this time it will not sink. So much energy is wasted by continually trying, without actually addressing the problem. So much energy can be saved and used in a much more beneficial manner if you sort the problem out to begin with, otherwise it will continually weigh you down.

On the little boat I show a sail. When the wind is still the boat does not move very fast. All it takes, my friends, is a little gust of the winds of change and the sail can be fully blown to its complete capacity. Within one second it takes off with great speed. I am aware that sometimes in your pathway of life, circumstances appear to be at a stand still. It is for you, while the boat is gently floating in the water going nowhere, for you to be on this boat. Look around, take in the beauty and the stillness that is there for you to look at, take in all that is around, the colour of the sky, the birds that fly. When you think your time is still, all things are there to be made the most of. You do not know when the winds of change shall come, before you know it you are off speeding down your pathway. You will find sometimes that there is very little time to take in the beauty around because you are so busy. This is why there is the time when things are calm, in order to recharge your batteries, to take in all that is there for you, so that when your boat takes sail you have inside all that you need because you have been preparing. Therefore as the boat sails so fast, you can enjoy the wind in your hair. You can enjoy the speed that you have been waiting for.

Also, I show now, that often when the winds have taken you far, it is up to you to drop the anchor. Sometimes it is necessary to take stock of what is happening so quickly. It is your decision to know when the anchor must go into the sand to keep you still for a little while in order again to take in what is around and to again recharge your batteries. I show that from the boat you take out of the little cupboard some food. It is necessary for you to be still and to take in the sustenance that you need, ready for the next part of your journey. If you did not prepare your soul for what lies ahead for you, then you would not be able to face your challenges with strength. Your energies would be weak. I realise that often it is very frustrating when there is a desire within your heart and there is nothing around that can fulfil this desire. As I spoke of before, it is around, it is merely waiting for your soul to be completely ready for when it comes to you.

I feel, because there are questions to be asked that might be in need of a longer answer, that it would be a good time to have my enjoyable time. Not that the rest is not! But I do enjoy the conversation between us all. I am aware that xxxx would like to ask a specific question and therefore I hand the floor over to you.

Its about drugs. How do you deal with someone and help someone who has a drug problem? Or is the problem actually not them, is it around them where the problem lies?

I show to Blossom what many would see as what you would imagine to be the peace pipe. All souls of this time are aware that souls in the lifetime that I last lived, were one of the same regarding the smoking of drugs. I show to Blossom that a soul of my lifetime was a particular soul that was chosen to go into the forest. This soul would know of the natural herbs that could come from plants and some berries and many different natural living plants. In our time there were certain herbs that would be hallucinatory. We specifically used these herbs to go in to our visionary dreamtime, to help another soul that required guidance. We would not, in our day, choose to smoke these herbs for the pure reason of sitting there completely 'off our heads' as you say, without a purpose. We used these for a sincere purpose. Sadly in the times that you are living your path much damage is done. The drugs that are smoked are not natural. They are not from the Divine Oneness. Also, they are abused. It is a sad fact that many young souls have lost their enthusiasm. They have found that by taking these drugs they can escape. Life then seems to be full of fun. As we are aware, for those who do not choose to take this form of escape, when you view this kind of fun, it really is not particularly funny. It is because they have lost their direction. It is not for another soul, my friends, to judge, or to condemn. It is free will. Regarding your question upon helping a soul, I show to Blossom a bucket on the sand. It is continually being filled until it is full, then patted down so that not one more grain can be packed in. When it is full, the activity must stop. It cannot continue, there is no more room. So the natural thing to do is empty out the bucket. It makes a mark, a shape in the sand. Then again the bucket is now empty and it can be refilled. There is a beach full of sand. One can choose to keep filling up the bucket if it wants, but after a while because there is so much, the enjoyment that one had of making these sand castles and forever filling oneself up, loses its pleasure. It becomes tedious. Where one could once make a pattern out of many buckets of sand, even to make a new pattern is no longer appealing. When that soul stands to look at the pattern it has created, it can see that it has really achieved nothing. When one is standing, as opposed to kneeling down, one looks at it from a different viewpoint. Then, suddenly the tide comes in and the waves wash away all that has been put into that particular project. The viewer can see that it has crumbled into nothing and the water flattens it out again. There is no longer the desire to start all over again. The viewer can see that it is fruitless, that it has achieved nothing. But, until the boredom of using this drug sets in, there is very little one can do to dissuade another not to take it. It is their path. Also, if it is the choice of another, but not for you, this does not mean that you have to continually put up with it. That is where you must look into your inner self to decide whether you care to deal with that situation. This does not mean, my friend, that you have to walk away. It means that you have to find a place of strength within yourself, so that it does not bother you, you do not allow it to bother you. If it is a choice to walk away because you cannot accept it, then that is your decision also. In some ways there are very little aspects to this smoking of this weed. Sometimes there is a little light bulb that comes into the soul, because it is a drug that can untie many knots inside. It is like with all things, that I'm sure you are aware, there are many things that are fine to be taken in small quantities. Leaving space in between until another small quantity can be enjoyed. It is when a soul abuses these things that they become harmful. Has that helped you in anyway?

Very much, thank you.

Often, as you know, what I say might not make a lot of sense at this particular time. As you are aware, the more you think it over, the more light will be shed upon it. Is there another question that I may be able to advise upon?

I wonder if there is any advice you could give us regarding helping more souls to find the Light and what messages should we be passing on to them?

I have to laugh xxxx ! Is it not that you spend every minute of your day doing this very thing! All whom you come across, you give messages to. All whom you come across, you give help to. So, although I understand what you are saying, there is so much that you do, that even if you were unaware of who may be joining us from ' the other side' this evening I am sure, that if the time comes when they would like you to pass on a message to their loved ones, you will do it without even knowing. It is so, that there are souls who have passed into the Summer Land, who choose also to come and join us because they have much to learn in the place where their soul is. This is welcomed by us in great gratitude. The more souls that myself and my band are able to assist on their pathway, then the greater the Light becomes as one. It is not that we require for ourselves for our Light to become brighter, but when we can brighten the soul of another, then the Light spreads. As it spreads, it connects up with the Light of others. Eventually, as the Oneness desires, we will become a Oneness of Light as we were in the beginning. Is there anything else because I feel am on a roll?

Laughter, then silence.

This is fine my friends. Before I take my leave, I am showing to Blossom that all around are many angels. They also have candles. The flame is so bright. It is because for souls such as mine and for much Higher souls as that of an angel, it is always a pleasure to the soul to be amongst the same Light. They are here in the four corners. It is that the Light from their candles is creating a line. It is as if you are encompassed all around by their Light. The Light between them is shining through into your very beings. It is an honour for us to be visited by such souls.

My friends, seeing that you do not have any more questions for me, it is time for me to take my leave. It is always a sort of sadness because I so enjoy being able to speak with you. I would like to say thank you, in front of you, to my friend Blossom, without her assistance I could not be heard.

We give thanks to the Divine Oneness for allowing this meeting to take place. We ask always that we may remain humble in order to serve and that we may continue to walk in the Light and the Love.

Thank you so much for your time and for your ears and for your laughter. Go peacefully my friends, until we may speak again.

Adieu, my friends, Adieu.

CHAPTER 21

The group took a break over the school holidays. On returning...

WHITE CLOUD: Welcome to you my friends.

We are more than a little surprised because of the time it took to reunite. It is amazing that when my energies have cleared away from Blossom totally, that we were so used to just accepting how easy it was. This evening we are connecting again. It is requiring far more concentration than originally thought. This, my friends, you can apply to many things that take place in your every day movements. There are so many things that one tends to take for granted. The simple act of walking, to one who has mobility in their legs, does not require much concentration, but to a soul who has lost the use of their legs and is learning to rebuild their automation, the concentration involved is phenomenal. It would do all of us no harm at all to concentrate a little more sometimes on the simple act of walking, to appreciate the knowledge of what takes place within your human body to accomplish such a movement. Also, my friends, it does one good to concentrate a little more sometimes on the very things that we do with such ease. In many circumstances we tend to take for granted what we are doing and we put our minds on something else. We feel with many things that we can do them standing on our heads and probably we can. If one was to remove complacency and put in the one hundred per cent concentration on these things that we can do blindfolded you would be quite surprised at the end result. It would be far more rewarding than usual.

I am showing to Blossom an image of a rolling pin and it is flattening out the pastry on a board. Around the edges where it has been rolled to the thinnest width possible, it has become frayed, it is not even, it is unappealing. In the centre where the concentration has been, that pastry looks even and thick. As it gets to the outside of this pastry, nobody would want to use this to make a pie, it looks so thin and lifeless. My friends, as you well know, if you were to put a pastry cutter into the middle and you cut out a simple square, all around the edges are little bits that are left over. Many people would tend to just gather them and throw them away because they are of no use. Those who desire to make the most out of all things would not consider to throw away these little bits. They know that if they gather them together they can start rolling and make something else. It is often, I show, that with a larger piece of pastry, it is put on top of the pie to finish off and put in the oven. If one perhaps fancies, they may take a fork and prick it so that it has a pattern. It is done without much thought at all. Whereas my friends, with the little piece that is left over, one has to think a bit more as to what can be done with it, what use can be got from it. So they would take the time to create a little pie that has fancy edges. It is a novelty. It is not something that is done every day. Because of the time and the concentration that is put into it, when that little piece of pastry comes out of the oven it is far more inviting than the big piece of pastry. So my friends, be careful of what you discard within yourself. Make sure that before you throw away completely what you feel to be of no use because it is thin and lifeless and uninviting, before you push it away from your life, have a little think to see that if perhaps you gathered all those loose ends together, you may perhaps discover a brand new talent.

It is, with many things, that people begin with enthusiasm. Sometimes, when the going gets tough, they let it lie. It can lie dormant never to be awakened. If you think of all these things that have been put by the wayside that once took your imagination to great heights, if they could be recaptured and put together, think of the discoveries that could unfold. There are so many things in a souls Earthly life that lie asleep for too long. The only reason that they are asleep is because the soul that put them to bed has never again told them that the sun has come up. Think about these things, my friends, it may take a little while for you to understand fully that which I speak. Know that it is so sad to see things wasted. To look down to your Earth and to view from our perspective, there are so many times when we would, if it was our way, pick you up like a money box and shake you. To wake you up, to say 'Can you not see what you are missing?' However that is not our duty - that is your job - wake yourself up!. Use all the facilities that lie in front of you.

I am showing to Blossom, there is a soul and all around it is a circle of... I need to say the word 'things'. It is as if it is positioned like a clock. You can pick any one up - it is within your grasp. All the way round there are so many things that are there for you to make the most of. So many of you prefer to use one or two, some, none at all, others use many. Look around you, feel around you, the minute you touch something or somebody that makes your fingers tingle do not ignore this sensation. When your body is set alight and awakened by a small thought, follow it through. It is your soul telling you that this is what it is needing to survive at this point. When I say survive I mean in the sense of 'to be kept alive'. One needs focus, my friends, this word, always remember this word. If one cannot find what to focus upon because there is no interest how can that soul survive? It has no food to keep it stimulated. Watch and listen, my friends, for the opportunities that are being presented to you everyday. Some are in disguise to make you think and to work things out for yourself and to use your mind that is so powerful. Others are so close to your face that it is almost squashing your nose, yet you still just ignore them. It is fear. Have the courage to face this thing that has come to you, that may be new. It is coming to you to tell you that the excitement that you long for, that you see in another souls life, is also there for you. Sometimes it cannot get any closer. It is your choice. As we have spoken before, take that leap, what have you to lose? If you are in a place where your soul is restless and unemployed what have you to lose? It requires also, people say in your world 'A leap of faith'. It is faith in yourself my friends that will ensure that when you jump you land safely. As we spoke once about the monkeys in the trees, once you have arrived because you have taken that leap, how stimulated you are with the new things around you. It is as if you have been reborn. You have new life. If you are not content where you are in yourself, move to a place where you are content. To live on your Earth plane on a day to day basis, with no enthusiasm and no Light to lead you, is pointless. It is in a sense, as if you might as well not be here. If the soul is sad and uncharged, what is one learning? What is one gaining? If the soul is alive then constantly it is receiving and giving Love, because of that Love, one can grow. This is why you have come to this Earth plane, to grow. If you are not going to feed yourself the water to help you to grow, then you simply will not. I apologise for digressing, Blossom is aware that when I speak of a flower being watered then I relate to a soul being Loved. It is for you to not wait for another soul to come with their watering can to feed your roots and lift you into the sunshine. It is for you to water your own roots, to give yourself all the Love that is there to take. It is an endless source. If you were to start everyday giving yourself this Love and allowing it to feed through to your roots and up your stem and into your very being, you would look forward to that watering. It would give you strength. Not only that, you would see that you were growing taller. You could see above the weeds that were blocking your view. That would give you encouragement to continue feeding yourself the water, because of the nourishment and the nurturing of yourself, because of the growth and the opening up of the petals allowing the sun to penetrate to the very centre of your flower. Once you have reached your full potential, then it is much easier for the overflow to be passed on to the flower that is growing next to you that is not so tall.

I am showing to Blossom an image of a wishing well that one throws coins into....

A long pause.

We will, with apologies, leave that there because we have broken the thread on that particular issue. Apologies are in order regarding this. It just goes to show that we are not perfect, that by the smallest lack of concentration how everything can fall apart. Perhaps that is why we allowed this to happen to show to you, that from where we started from, regarding this concentration, by not fully giving your hundred per cent, one slip could cause a landslide, my friends. Do not take for granted what is so easy to you, always give thanks for what you have been given, appreciate all you have. As I am sure you are aware that to another soul, simple tasks are nowhere near as easy. It is so important to give thanks for all your blessings. Some days, one may feel a little low. Their hearts desire is to have a certain item or a certain feeling that they cannot pick up upon that day. It may be a little hard to see what there is to give thanks for when one is of that frame of mind. My friends, that is the best time to give thanks and count your blessings for all you do have. Again it is so easily taken for granted. Becoming aware of all that you do have can lift your frame of mind also. As you know, because of natural law, by giving thanks for what you have and who you are, this automatically brings to you all the others, the desires that you requested.

One was speaking to Blossom today as to where I might have gone. I show to Blossom the sunshine and that I went to the very centre of that sun. Believe me, where I retired to, was very, very, warm for my soul. I show myself under a waterfall because I am totally refreshed. It is a good thing my friends to get away for a while, one can then see things from a different perspective just by having a little break and recharging the batteries. It is wonderful to be back with you, there are new aspects that can now be introduced as we progress.

If I may, before I go, say to the lady sitting next to me that I show to Blossom a wood fire. You are warming your hands because the Light around you feels cold and you feel that you need to warm yourself up. I would like you to think upon this, that all of the night sky is beautiful and to sit around the log fire warming yourself is an experience, but there are other ways for you to get warm. Perhaps by walking in the sunshine, in the daylight, might be another way for you to get the warmth that you require.

We give thanks to the Divine Oneness for allowing this meeting to take place. We ask always that we may remain humble in order to serve and that we may continue to walk in the Light and the Love.

Adieu, my friends, Adieu.

CHAPTER 22

WHITE CLOUD. A warm welcome to you my good friends.

There is so much energy that is flowing between us that I feel I could burst. I am showing to Blossom immediately that it is as if there is a birthday party being held here because there is so much to celebrate. It is that you are all at this same party. I show that on your birthday table there is a jug of liquid that is strawberry in flavour. In it now, I show on the top, many beautiful pink rose petals that are delicately manoeuvring themselves around the top of this fluid. From there I show a small whirlpool is transcending down this fluid to the bottom of the jug. As the momentum builds to the point at the bottom of the jug the rose petals are sucked in and down. You can suddenly see them no more, they have disappeared in this little tornado. I then show that this little storm builds up and builds up and builds up and all of a sudden it spits out again these petals. Now they are not pink. They are pure white. The water now is clear. My friends, sometimes it is necessary for some part of your being to be almost sucked under until you feel that maybe you have lost it forever. The whirlpool that sucked it under feels that it is spinning so fast it makes you dizzy and you shall fall. It is as if sometimes this whirlpool has brought you to screaming point. It is only then when you can no longer even grasp where it has gone, when you can no longer see it, it is then that the transformation is taking place. It is like in a magic show when something disappears and 'Hey presto' it has suddenly transformed into something completely different. This is why I show that when the white petals have risen like the phoenix from the fire, that what is reborn, what is renewed is the outcome. What then lies on the top of the clear water is the beauty that should now be seen. There was nothing ugly about the rose coloured water and the pink petals. It is just that it is time for a change. When a change is taking place it is necessary for this turmoil and the stirring up of all things. The shift that you have been talking of can take place. It is as if you can imagine that sand is on the bottom of the jug, if this whirlwind did not take place the sand would stay the same. All the grains of sand would remain next to the same grain of sand that it has been next to for a long time. With this stirring up it makes the sand rise. If you look into the jug for a while it is cloudy and murky and not attractive to the eye at all. When the whirlwind begins to slow down because it has reached its peak, then how differently all the little grains of sand settle. They settle next to a different grain of sand. My friends, do you not see that all this sand has always been part of the same group in the same jug. Now because of the change required, when it is settled it is still part of the same group, except that it has somebody new to talk to so life isn't so boring looking out of the same piece of glass! I think really I have spoken enough about the jug situation. It is because I am aware that for many souls who are gaining their spiritual strength, and as you spoke, you are aware of this change, that I wanted to explain to you what is taking place and why souls feel this turmoil. Like all things, when the dust has settled, how nice it is to view the world with fresh eyes and from a different place. When your 'shift' has completely taken its fullness then you will be very aware of the degree necessary in order to find yourself in such a beautiful land.

I show then that the white petals are taken out of the jug and they are arranged in little posies and wrapped in silver foil. It is the simplicity that makes anything find its beauty. One could go to enormous extremes and design ribbons and bells, many, many things to wrap around these white petals, but by doing so, it shifts the focus to the ribbons and the paraphernalia and by doing so it takes the eye away from the simple beauty of the white petal. Therefore just to wrap it in something that does not take away the attention from where it belongs is the point that I am trying to make to you.

It is often that one likes to dress up and this is fine .Do not allow what you are wearing to take up the attention because the beauty does not lie there. The beauty lies in the sparkle of your eyes.

My throat had become very dry as it often does during these sessions

Now then, this might be a bit of a laugh because Blossom is in serious need of a drink of water! We have not yet tried this experiment. So I wonder if somebody could kindly pass the glass for her to sip from?

The glass was handed to me and I drank. It took me by surprise as my entire body reacted by trembling. I guess White Cloud hadn't had a drink for quite a while!

Now we are adjusting the retinas of the eyes. It is an accomplishment if I am able to look into the eyes of another. At the moment it is something that is requiring much concentration because there will be an effect that takes place when this happens. It can be quite traumatic for the body and I believe there has been enough of that for the moment. I would like to work my way towards this. It is that it is for the permission of my young male friend xxxx that I may use him to look in his eyes. You need xxxx to prepare yourself, it is not that it is to be scary, it is that this is the way it is without going into volumes of detail. It is also a lot of concentration for us. You see it is a vital part of my work for this contact to expand, by looking into another's eyes there is much that can be seen from one to another. By being able to do this it will aid my work greatly. It would be an honour for me if it would be your eyes xxxx that I look into.

When White Cloud had opened his eyes in the past there had been no actual eye contact made with another. So once again excitement in the air for a new experience. Much deep breathing and energy was built up. Xxxx prepared his body by surrounding it with Love and Light. Eventually White Cloud opened my eyes. He gradually brought his vision nearer to where xxxx was sitting. He then looked at his chest. It took quite a while before my eyes were able to look into xxxx. When they did there was an overwhelming sense of Love. Xxxx was beaming at White Cloud. It was difficult to continue as White Cloud was overcome with emotion. As I am listening to the tape now, tears are falling. His voice was shaking and broken. It was a real moment for not just White Cloud and I , but for everyone present.

Welcome my friend. You are a good boy! It is an experience and I thank you. Well now, where do we go from here?

You see that I am able, my friends, now to be with you. It is that I am here now. It is something that is very strange because Blossom is still here as well. We are joined fully as one in order to do this. Mr. Goody are you looking my friend? Are you all right? because this must be strange that I am your wife!

Much laughter.

I know you are very understanding and it is very much that you were chosen. You chose also to be with Blossom in order for you to accept these gifts and to be able to go along with us. Although you wonder why because you feel that your gifts are not fully displayed to another. It is that it was a very special man that was needed to be with Blossom. You are that soul. You go about your business in silence. Your time Mr. Goody will be open to you very shortly. It is essential for you to be as you are at this time. Blossom is finding it hard to look at you. Blossom that is in there *(pointing to my head)* because of the complete idiocy of this whole thing!

Again much laughter

You see my friends, now I can speak with you. I can look at you and we can talk more on a one to one level. You must forgive that I have not much prepared, it is a phenomenon in itself that this is taking place. Now that it has, it is the first step up a very tall ladder. Much, now that we are on the first rung my friends, can be accomplished by us. It is strange for us, for the eyes not to be closed, that is how we have worked for so long. Everything... Blossom is saying to me 'I can't say this,' but I can and I will.... that everything is arse about face!

Guess what? More laughter

That is how it is my friends because it is that it is a new phenomenon as I have said. Just in itself for us it is something that I have worked upon for a long, long time. It is something that for Blossom is also very new.

Now as I said, I had perhaps better concentrate because I do not know what to do for the first time. My friends I would like to say in all sincerity that it is a dream come true for me to accomplish this moment. It is also very much because of your Love and the Love from Blossom that I can do this. You would not yet be able to understand the eons of time that this has been planned. When you look into the fact that it has been planned to be with you sitting there and you there and so on. This was put into being a long, long time ago when you did not even have these particular bodies. It is that these are the bodies you chose to be in. When it was shown that this would be, you were in your spirit form. That was all that was necessary at that time, I hope that you are all happy with what you have chosen. You chose it for one reason or another so I say to you that if this is your choice then get on with it and be happy with it. You chose it to express exactly who you are. It is that when you are not happy with it, merely look at the things, the issues that come about because of your unhappiness with it. If you were to correct all those things, then you would look in the mirror and whether you were gigantic or minute you would Love what you saw.

I feel now that I have done my party piece.

It is time for me to take my leave, after today's experience, believe me, I will fly home on my wings. I am aware of ninety million birthday presents that I have opened this evening for myself. Many, many thanks my friends, you do not, or maybe only part of you does, understand the enormity of this accomplishment.

We give thanks to the Divine Oneness for allowing this meeting to take place. We ask always that we may remain humble in order to serve and that we may continue to walk in the Light and the Love.

Adieu, my friends, Adieu.

CHAPTER 23

WHITE CLOUD. Good afternoon to you my friends.

A moment was taken and energy built up so that White Cloud could open his/my eyes. He stared into the candle flame.

You see when one has discovered a party trick then they like to use it over and over to appeal to the crowds. It is that I am more comfortable now with the eyes open.

xxxx, is it agreeable with you to make the connection with the eyes today? because I can not concentrate until I can talk as one to another. You understand to brace yourself for the moment of contact. You will know when you are 'switched on' enough.

Much deep breathing took place and eventually he looked directly into xxxx eyes. There is always much emotion involved for him at the moment of eye contact and this in turn fills me with that emotion. Quite tricky sometimes to keep ones decorum!

Many thanks my friend. It is that, I find it to be rude if I do not do now what I know I can do. It is for me, that I like to speak with you in this manner. It is my friends that I require for a connection to be made with the young lady in the blue and I would like to work around the group. I do not wish to leave anybody out. But for the new comers, for me, it is difficult for the vibration... If you wouldn't mind, for there to be a joining of hands.

At this point White Cloud was able to make eye contact with the souls in the group who had been there the previous night, but when he tried to do the same with the members who had not been present, we found that the energy was unable to blend and his voice would go peculiar and gasps of breath were taken.

Please do not take offense at all, to the new people. It is that my vibration is affecting the body because of the difference in energies. It is that for the new eyes, to build around themselves, if you would, an imaginary Light that my vibration can then connect up with yours, at the moment it is too much of a difference. So, if you can, imagine connecting yourself, your etheric body, your outer self, to blend in with that which is around mine and Blossoms. It is like smoke and it is merging into one piece of smoke and then it won't be such a difference. My friends, there is nothing to fear, it is a mere question of blending with each other and then we can get started.

xxxx can you open your eyes when you feel ready.... Welcome to you my friend!

Again much emotion. The lady concerned had been to many meetings and Loved him dearly, but the actual contact with the eyes is like a soul connection. White Cloud and the soul's eyes he is looking into cannot help but be overwhelmed with emotion - an extraordinary feeling.

For you xxxx, do not look so forlorn, I was not taking you separately from the others you understand. Now all that is left is for xxxx, and your turn is coming! I need you to close your eyes and when you feel it is all right with you, to slowly look into mine and if you could do it slowly otherwise I may jump through the chair! That is fine, it was just a little flutter for me and are you well? You look like you do sometimes, Blossom is saying, when your eyes will pop out your head. I welcome you my friends and now perhaps we can get on with the matter today.

It was that Blossom was asking me, when there was the silence to start, 'What it is that I want?'. It is my friends, that I ask you to look at what it is that YOU want. It is important for you to find what it is you want. It is not something that you

VIP

think 'Oh maybe one day I would like this.', it is essential to have a plan for yourselves and to know that plan is your Truth. When you have that, then your plan and your Truth are set into motion, because that plan was drawn out before you came. It is a matter of recalling your plans so that when your time is finished at this plane you will not arrive somewhere else without all the shopping you had gone out for! Sometimes it is that you arrive somewhere else in your journey, you have a basket full of shopping but sometimes you get there and you have different ingredients from what you originally went to buy. It is that sometimes you can make use of these other ingredients which you did not realise you wanted. Since you have them, use them. It is that others are completely useless for your designs. It is that, the things you find in your bag that are of no use, they have been a weight that you have carried unnecessarily, you need not have paid money for them and at a very high cost sometimes. Look at what is in your shopping bag, you will find that there are certain things in there that you knew, when you left, were imperative that you came home with. Always make sure that you have bought those things. It is my friends, that when you get to another place you realise that there is not a bus back for a long time to those shops so how can you get those things you require? It is best to make your list clear before you go. Then you will not forget the things that you really need in this journey that you are making. You may feel that sometimes, and I speak with you xxxx of your singing, you know in your heart that is your plan. You have tried No. 29 bus and you have tried No.16. They did not take you to where you needed to be. Don't stop, get a taxi! Do you see? - there are ways. When it hurts your heart, it will be when you arrive, and all the shopping that 'singing supermarket' could give you, is not there. It has only a few bits and bobs. It is for you, in your singing because it is your soul, that you need a trolley full. When you sing you will bring about all the things you need in your trolley. Do not wait as one can, over and over for that bus to arrive as we know sometimes, they don't! You need to concentrate and make it happen. It is not enough my friends to think 'One day that would be nice.' - that is not enough, it must be focussed my friends and put down so that it can be ticked when it has come to you. These desires, these gifts, these talents inside of you are not there to be trapped. They are there and as with your drawings, as with your singing, as with all your different talents they were 'put in' because not every soul can have them all otherwise they would explode. It is therefore, that they have been shared out amongst everyone, to give to others. If you do not bring it forth in yourself, you are not only denying yourself, you are denying others the beauty that you were given. One feels doubt inside because perhaps with your drawings, you see another's drawings and you feel 'I don't know if I could do as well,' You do not want to do as well, you want to do better than what you see. As your heart is pulling you to paint, especially, my friends with gifts of the Arts, when you can be stirred and stir others with that gift, do not waste your time and energy wondering if it would be any good. If it is calling you, it is calling you for a reason. It is your connection. It is for each one of you to know inside what your gifts are and not to let them sleep all your life, but to waken them. It is NOW that this quickening takes place. As you know, if it is a thought it can become a reality so quickly. Time is quickening up so do it NOW, do not sit at home watching your television thinking 'Oh well, I'll think about it' and another five years has gone by. You are denying, all around you, five years of your gifts.

I stress to you my friends concerning the route you take. That is what you all must look at. One is so easily stopped in their tracks by disappointment, by a blockage in the flow. Pull out the plug! Let it flow again! When you put these blockages on yourself, you cannot see the effects of energy around that you have placed. When you speak of putting a brick wall up, indeed that is what you are doing. For that energy of creativity to flow in and then come out, how difficult is that for it to flow through a brick wall? Don't knock it down, just don't put it there in the first place!

There are a lot of souls that do not know what it is. They say 'But I can't do anything. You can do this and this but I have nothing to give'. It is because they did not go to the shops my friends and look at what they could buy. They do not look at all the shelves for opportunities. They look in one little corner shop. If they cannot find what is appealing to eat that day, they come home hungry, they do not venture to another shop where there is more choice to be opened up to them. Take these people and show them where the supermarkets are. Give them the opportunity of choice. For those who are lost, it is that they have dropped their little plan. They don't know where to find it. If one puts them on their path, it is as if they can put it down on paper all over again, because the memory is coming back to them. They realise that it is not just the one road, there are many paths they can take, but they had not looked to see if they were there.

Live your lives, my friends, while you are upon this Earth plane. Do not waste one moment. Here you can gain so much knowledge so quickly. It is not as easy on other planes. You are very fortunate to be here at this time. So use it. Use it. Do not abuse it.

My friends, that is all for me to say today because it requires a lot more energy than before. One must take it a bit at a time to adjust for Blossom's sake. You are aware that to look into another's eyes is the way to the soul. That is how another can feel your Love in all levels of soul to soul contact. It is sometimes, when you look in one's eyes, that you see a long staircase to get to that soul. If you keep climbing upwards, eventually you will get to the place you need to be to say hello on the level you require. You will find then that you do not need to walk back, there is an elevator to bring you back so quickly. With all efforts regarding touching another's heart there is reward. I am aware that one does not give Love in order to receive a reward, but the Divine Oneness will give you a gift for your efforts as Natural Law.

We give thanks for allowing this meeting to take place. We ask always that we remain humble in order to serve and that we continue to walk in the Light and the Love.

My friends, it is an honour for me to look into the eyes of your souls. You understand that I would not be able to do so, if the eyes were not filled with great Love.

Adieu, my friends, Adieu.

CHAPTER 24

This meeting took place in a friend's garden. I was guided to a large tree and felt White Cloud wanted me to stand with my back against it. The rest of the group sat around on chairs. It was a sunny day but there was a pleasant breeze. White Cloud took a long time to come through. When he did he opened his eyes and immediately he and I were filled with emotion. He had not experienced a blue sky through human eyes in a long time.

WHITE CLOUD. I apologise for the delay, but as I spoke with Blossom before hand, there is something afoot. Blossom is needing me to say that she knows that you can trust what she is doing and that she needs your Love on this one.

There then took place incredibly deep breathing, controlled by him. I had the feeling he wanted me to stand and was not sure that I could! Trust! Giving it a go, it happened! There he was standing - I felt a foot taller all round!

As a baby takes its first steps, you can now amuse yourselves at my wobbling! It is my desire to reach inside each one of you. xxxx you can be the bravest one because there is nothing to fear. You can now help me with your energy to get over to you. Also my friends, I need you to visualise my attachment to this tree. This is where my cord is connected to keep me and all where they should be at the end of this experiment. So please visualise the attachment because it is important.
It is good to have my feet on the ground.

When he had built up enough energy, he slowly walked over to xxxx. It is very difficult to describe the feeling, an odd sensation of experiencing the new - from my viewpoint and his. He put his hand on her head.

I give to you xxxx the gift of Light. As the eagle flies, so shall your spirit be free. It is good to feel the wind in my hair.

At this point I had to control my emotions, as the experience of the wind in his hair, for him, was overwhelming. I could feel exactly what he was feeling. It was a beautiful moment we shared. Thank you! He then moved on to the next soul and repeated the procedure.

I give to you, my special Queen, the gift of Peace. Peace you shall have and Peace you shall bring..

Again moving on:

I give to you xxxx the gift of earth. Where your roots are planted miracles shall grow.

Moving on, there was then another burst of 'energy breathing'. He put his right hand up directly towards the sun and then placed it upon xxxx head.

And to you xxxx, I give you the power from the sunlight. Know now that it is inside, it shall never deplete, so it can be given freely to all who come into your presence.

And I give a gift to myself - to stand in this sunshine.

His voice became very emotional and his tears fell down my cheeks. Each soul present said afterwards that they experienced an incredible peace and Love flowing through them. Apparently there was not a dry eye in the house!

Now I must go back in the route I came so as not to get tangled up but while I am here...

He once again stood in the silence and appreciated the moments he had, to feel the beauty of just being on this planet. The birds were singing, the sun was shining, a gentle breeze blew - what more could a guy want!

As he retraced back to the tree, xxxx asked him if she could give him a hug.

I feel my friend, that it is not possible, because it is too much. We can work on it that one day this may be so.
I must go home. It has been phenomenal. Thank you my friends.

All a little overwhelmed. When he'd gone, I opened my eyes. All a little blown away!

As I let the tape run on, when transferring it to this page, I heard me say 'Ground control to Major Tom'. An excellent day. A magical experience for us all. Above all I felt so honoured to be able to experience such a wonder.

CHAPTER 25

WHITE CLOUD. A warm welcome to you my dear friends.

I am showing to Blossom the image of a parachute coming out of a plane with a human being attached, drifting back and forth through the winds of change. It is my friends, that sometimes when a parachute is not caught by the wind, it can feel as if one is falling rapidly out of control. A little fear and doubt comes into that being. My friends, put your trust in the winds of change. Just as you feel that you are falling at a rate that is unappealing to you, out of nowhere a gust of wind will catch your parachute and take you soaring higher once again. With that gust comes upliftment. You find then, that things feel calmer. You feel safer. You realise that you are not going to plummet to the ground. Allow your wings to take you higher. Sometimes it seems as if one is lifted, then loses the flow of the wind and is falling again. It is only the weight of yourselves that pulls you down. Know that even when you cannot feel the breeze, it is only just around the corner.

I show now, many people in the air with their parachutes. When you look upon this phenomenon I am sure that when you are in the air, you see others before the parachute has opened and it would seem an impossibility for each of you to join up and hold hands in a circle, in such a place, with so many elements going against this. What you must know my friends, is even when sometimes it seems as if you are far away from the others, the force of Love will bring you together in a circle of Love, no matter where or what the circumstances. It is always that, even if the circle of people felt they were falling, one always feels more secure if you are all falling together than to be falling on your own. I show that some parachutes may catch the wind, because of their position, earlier or later than others. When one is able to look above and see that another is higher, when they had once been on the same level, it gives hope. Always to trust. I desire to speak of this word trust.

I show, because I have not spoken of food for a long time.... I show a single piece of bread. To your eyes you see the piece of bread. If you put it into your toaster, when it has finished 'warming up', to your eye it looks very different. Your knowing of the Truth is that it is still that same piece of bread, it just looks different. Then one can place on top some butter and then I show what Blossom would call Marmite but it is different in your country. There again you are looking at that same piece of bread, but now it looks transformed from its original guise. It matters not what something appears to be. It matters only what it is. If you were to taste the plain slice of bread, it would taste very different from when it was transformed. Ultimately you are absorbing the same thing. What I say is, because you saw the slice of bread in its original form and it was you that brought about the transformation, you do not need to trust that it is the same piece of bread, because you know! It is, I am aware my friends, far more difficult to know of the true form of something when it has been changed without your knowledge. How can you? In simplistic terms, if you had not seen that bread before it was buttered and toasted, how could you be sure that once it was completely different.?

To Trust requires courage. To Trust does not require knowledge, it merely requires TRUTH. As I have said, what you as yourself know yourself to be, is where your Trust must come from. It maybe, as I know my friends is happening for some of you, that there is questioning regarding this Truth that one feels. It is good to have this questioning and this doubt sometimes. When it is through, you know your Truth. If when you ask yourself certain questions, you arrive at an answer that is surprising to you, but it settles for you, then that is your

Truth. Do not be of concern that it is not the answer you thought you would get. Maybe, that was your Truth originally, but it has changed its form. It has more butter on now. It tastes a little more luscious. Truth, my friends, is the same. It is always the same slice of bread, it sometimes appears different from what you originally thought, that is all. It elaborates itself.

To return to the subject of Trusting, I am well aware how difficult at times this can be. When things are not as you would desire them to be it is sometimes difficult to 'know' that the outcome will be of the picture that you paint. Notice, if you would, that I do not choose to use the word 'believe' I choose the word to 'know'. There is a vast difference in believing and knowing. If you believe something, beliefs can change. If you truly know something - it cannot.

When I resided upon your Earth plane, there were times when the vegetation was not always as fruitful as one would desire for ones families. We did not go into a panic, as sadly some of your farmer's etc do, we knew, and I will say again 'All is as should be'. We did not concern ourselves of famine. We trusted completely that The Oneness of All was on our side. Whatever way at that time we were to live our daily lives, did not change because of the vegetation not growing as we desired. We did not become effected by what was taking place around us. What was in us was solid Truth - there was no doubt that The Creator would wish us harm. There was Trust always. My friends, I can feel sometimes for you, how in this society, it can become difficult. You cannot teach yourself to know, you cannot teach yourself to Trust, you already know how to do it. You must allow yourself to know, allow yourself to Trust. These times when you sometimes feel that you have, not a 'white cloud' over you, but a grey cloud that is raining just above your head, not anybody else's, perhaps the rain that is coming down are the tears that you are flowing. They need to be released in order to give you more freedom of yourself. If you notice, when a cloud is full of rain it has the appearance of greyness and heavy weight. When it has released all that it is burdening itself with, it can become, like me, nice and fluffy! It can lift itself because it has no weight anymore. It can, when you look in the sky, appear completely different. Its weight has been released. Always my friends you can know, that if this is upon your head, be assured that a gust of wind will come when it is the most valuable time and simply blow it away for you, to reveal once again the warmth of the beautiful sunshine.

I show to Blossom that it is for souls sometimes as if they have put big heavy boots on, that have lead weights planted in the bottom of them. Sometimes it feels so hard to stride just the smallest of paces. It is so much hard work. Sit down and take your boots off! Then, when you have removed the problem, you will find that you have light fairy feet, you do not have to even consider the movement required, everything once more is Light. It is necessary sometimes to walk a little way with these boots on before the penny drops. If you had not experienced the weight of these heavy boots, how could you enjoy the dancing on the fresh grass in bare feet?

These highs and lows come to you, my friends, for your development. They help you when you use that situation wisely, to understand who you are. Many people say 'this is where I'm at.'- it matters not where you are at, it matters who you are. If you are in your happiness, in your peace, it matters not where you are because you will still be in the right place. If you are in a wrong place, I do not like to use that word 'wrong', I choose to use the words 'a more uncomfortable place' within your self, you could be in the most beautiful surroundings, but you could not feel their Love. Yet at another time my friends, to be sombre for a moment, regarding the tragedies in the land of the Americans (Sept 11th), if one is in a place of Love within themselves and they are giving Love, they will not see the devastation, they will only see the good that is coming out of this situation.

I wish to say to you all, do not pat yourself on the head and dig yourself down in the ground, pat yourself on the back. Remind yourselves how far you have come on this journey of yours. I know that for each soul in this room, if you were to remind yourselves of, first of all, five of your years ago, what were your thoughts and your knowing then? Then look to three years ago, you had changed a little, then two of your years, then my friends, look back to two of your weeks. You are continually expanding the expression of yourselves. Do not forget about this. One, when in a place of joy and Love, can sometimes so easily find that acceptable. I am not saying that you do not give gratitude for your blessings. When one is in a happy disposition, you just enjoy laughing. You allow yourself to do so. You do not question 'Why am I so happy?' so why do you do it when you are feeling a little low? Allow it to take its form. Do not punish yourselves because you feel it is not quite the right thing. It is the difference of the boots and the bare feet, the low feeling and the high feeling. You must have the two to know the difference.

Now I wonder if after such a long time you have done your homework and you have a question prepared for me?

Silence ensued!

I have a question for you, I do not require the answer. I would desire you to answer it for yourselves inside yourself. If I was to ask you on a scale of one to ten where you would place yourself regarding yourself, what number would you give? If you are to give yourself a number on the lower scale, then I suggest you do something immediately to change that. Do not feel if you would like to give yourself nine or ten that it would be wrong. I use that word again! Perhaps you would be concerned regarding your big headedness. If you can give yourself your number in your Truth, then you can know what it is you desire to work towards. If you choose to give yourself ten out of ten, then I give you a gold star. You have worked hard to get your results. I say to many souls, 'DO NOT UNDERESTIMATE WHO YOU ARE!'

It would be interesting if you were able to see yourselves without your bodies. Would you look at another friend and say 'Oh, I did not realise you were so bright'. Would you look at them and think 'Oh, I did not realise you are not so bright as I thought you were!' You see my friends, when there is nothing but your Light you would see for yourselves how beautifully Lit Up you are. You cannot be that bright unless you have earned your Light so please, I ask you to recognise yourselves. You all look at one another in Love. As Blossom says, in this group that she is with here, never is there a word against another, you all give and receive Love. Try to look at yourselves as others see you, they treat you as they do because they know who you are, you know who they are. Know that you are part of that circle of the parachutes in the sky. Know also that there will be many times when the wind comes and lifts you higher together, so high, my friends, that you will need oxygen masks.

Try not to think of the more challenging times as a struggle, try to find the Love, in and around, even when it is looking a little murky outside of yourself. Do whatever it is that comes to you. Perhaps you might need to get a hoover and blow it all away. Perhaps you might get a duster and dust it away. Visualisation is a very powerful tool. As the medicine men of my day worked shamanically in that way, it will work just as easily for you. Whatever situation is not feeling comfortable, look at it and then change it into something you can deal with visually. If you are having conflict with others, change those others to be a messy food table. Watch yourself tidy it all up and make everything look nice again. It will have the same effect on the matter, you are bringing about change. All you have to do is put Love into tidying up that table and removing the crumbs and the mess. By now, my friends, you know that it is Love and only Love that one needs for everything, for everyone. How bright the world would be if each soul had this knowledge, not only had it, but used it.

I have enjoyed so much once again my discourse with you.
We give thanks to the Divine Oneness for allowing this meeting to take place. We ask always that we may remain humble in order to serve and that we may continue to walk in the Light and the Love.

My friends, take off your boots if they are too heavy, skip and dance in the freedom of yourself.

My Love as always surrounds you and penetrates your soul.

Adieu, my friends, Adieu.

CHAPTER 26

This meeting took place outside.

WHITE CLOUD: A very warm welcome to you all.

I am showing to Blossom the image of the red rose. We must apologise to you because we are having a little trouble because of the insects that are trying to join in today!

I am showing that in the centre is a beautiful red rose that is closed. Either side are white roses that are also closed. I show that the white roses open up in the glory of the sunshine. The red rose is aware that these roses that are white are different from itself. They have already come into their fullness. I show that the red rose is trying with all its might to blossom into itself, into its full capacity. However hard it is forcing itself to do so, it cannot budge the outer petals, they are clamped firmly where they belong at that time. I show that because of this, the red rose in the centre is beginning to curl under and loose its strength. It feels that because it is in the centre it should be the one that stands out amongst the others. It is different. It feels it should be the one to be valued by others. The ones either side are instead showing their beauty, and the red rose begins to lose its life force. It begins to curl under and wither. I show that eventually it is lying upon the ground. Where its roots are, there is no water at all. Whereas the white roses are surrounded by their food of Love, by their water. They are filled because of this Love. Gradually the water from either side is seeping through the soil to the place where the red rose bud lies. Gradually the red rose bud can feel this Love coming to it. The more it begins to pick itself up, the more it is able to absorb water from either side from the white roses. There is a time when because the red rose is taking the water from the white roses, the white roses begin to, for a little while, loose their vitality. They are giving so much to another that needs the Love at that time. I show that this rose grows taller than the two white roses. The red rose soars above them. They now look a little weak and not so pure as they had done before. It is then, when it is at its fullest height, that the red rose comes into itself and opens up. As it does so, each morning, the dew that is upon its petals is able to drip off onto the white roses and feed them with the same Love. It is my friends, this thing with Love. Sometimes one does not feel that it is being given enough. One feels depleted and that one is sinking too fast and does not have the strength to get up. If you look around you, you will always find that either side, that anyway you look, when you are at your lowest there will always be some white roses that are stronger than you at that time. They will happily give of their Love to you in order to pick you up again. When they have brought you back into the rose that you should be, then you can return that kindness. It is a never ending circle my friends.

I show that behind these roses there is a white fence. Although one would like to grow higher and higher up into the sunshine, to be closer to the warmth, it is necessary sometimes for the roses to intertwine themselves amongst the panels of the fence. So, instead of taking all the sunlight to themselves, they are prepared to spread their beauty out along the fence. In this way, when they open each morning and their dew falls, it can fall upon other little flowers that are along the fence, flowers that had thought they had no chance of receiving any of the water for themselves. Then they can also grow. They can too spread themselves amongst the fences and so it goes my friends. As you know, it is important for you to work with the Love you have. It is fine to feel it within yourself and give Love with your mind and your thought to the Great Oneness. Sometimes it maybe that, because you are giving so much thanks out there, you may be failing to catch sight of the little bud in the ground further along the fence. A little bud that is yearning for your attention and for your Love. Do not, my friends, just look straight ahead, look either side and all around you. You are wise souls, try to expand your Love in new ways and further afield.

As I show further down the fence there are other flowers that have had much water. It is, that when you are able to give Love to these little ones that are struggling, as you go further along, you will come across every now and then, a flower that stands proud and strong. It knows itself. When you meet these flowers you will in turn be given new strength and new wisdom from these flowers that you may not have looked upon in that way before. So many souls have blinkers upon their eyes, they look only forward in one direction. Remember that if you walk down one pathway and there are others to travel, that they will come to the same place in the end. It may take you a little longer to go round this way but think of the experiences and learning and Love that you can gain along the way.

I show that along a bricked pathway there are little weeds that are growing out of the cracks from where the bricks have been laid. One would not think that it would be easy for weeds and flowers to grow once these heavy bricks have been placed upon them, that there would be any possibility of this life force coming through such a concrete solid mass. You can see my friends, that all things can grow through anything. You may find sometimes that you are up against a brick wall. When you are faced with a wall that you feel you cannot possibly penetrate through, it seems like it will never go away. Think of these little weeds and the little daisies. How minute, how delicate they are. Because of their determination and because of their knowledge, they can come through this stone wall. So know that when you are faced with this wall that will not go away, do not try to knock it down, but think of your Love that can penetrate through anything and bring you through to the other side.

Blossom was just saying that these ants might not bother

me but they are bothering her! They will leave my friends. They will leave.

And they did.

I am showing to Blossom now an image of the swing she was upon earlier today. Sometimes one is happy just to sit upon the swing and for it not to move at all. One does not feel inclined to make the slightest bit of effort in the movement to get the momentum going. That is fine. If one needs to sit and contemplate in the stillness then that is what one must do. You will find my friends, that sometimes when you sit on a swing, however much you would like to stay still, there is something within you that just begins to rock. The more you rock just a little bit, the more the momentum gathers. Keep at the desired pace that is comfortable for yourself. It maybe that when you have swung, just a little while, that you need to be still again, so do so. When you are ready, you will find yourself again on the pendulum of life. As it gently moves forward and back you will find that you gain your own rhythm.

I show that on the swing that is next to the one I speak of, there is another soul that is swinging very high. It is making the other soul feel rather sick. Do not try and take on where another is at. One feels sick because one is imagining and taking on board how another is feeling. It is not for you to do so. Remain firmly within yourself and your own pendulum. Often you know, the soul that you thought was on a tremendous high, full of life and 'joie de vivre', actually might look at you and think that it looks rather peaceful down there. It might gradually slow itself down to come and be in alignment with you. Then maybe when you have gained the same balance and the same rhythm, you will decide that you would like to go higher with this other soul and you can do so in synchronization. You will not be feeling this nauseous feeling, you are too busy being happy that you are in the same rhythm as another soul.

What I say to you my friends, is something that I have said to you in many ways before, be at peace with yourself and where you are. If you try to become where another is, when your place is not there, you will feel confused, bound up, tense and nauseous. Be at peace with where you belong. Do not try to reach another's height. Allow another to come down to you and gently take you with them, in balance together.

The time has come once again to take my leave.

We give thanks to the Divine Oneness for allowing this meeting to take place. We ask always that we may remain humble in order to serve and that we may continue to walk in the Light and the Love.

Adieu, my friends, Adieu.

CHAPTER 27

This meeting took place after the September 11th disaster. It was a short meeting. White Cloud explains the reasons for this.

WHITE CLOUD: A very warm welcome to you all my dear friends.

I am showing to Blossom an image of a bunch of beautiful red tulips. Then I show that they change to the colour of black velvet tulips. You know my friends, that one tends to look upon the colour black to mean darkness and things that are of a sad nature. For instance, when a soul in your world attends a funeral it is for them to be in mourning and wear black. Whereas in our realm we are there to greet them in an array of bright colours. If you were to look upon a black velvet tulip you would immediately be in awe of its beauty. So it is my friends, that when things appear to be black to you, it is also, as in all things that there is the balance, the opposite.

This is what I desire to speak with you regarding what you call a terrible tragedy that took place in your world not long ago. It is my friends, that because you cannot be in the place that I am reviewing the situation from, that you cannot see also the benefits. I realise that to use the word 'benefit' when such sorrow has befallen many thousands of souls, that you might find this word to be obtrusive. We all know there are other reasons behind the sorrow in order for the Light to shine through. It is a fact that many advanced souls from our world were already in position to come to the aid of the souls that required assistance. The pre-destiny was already accounted for. Do not misunderstand. It was not that what took place was one of elation by any means. In our world much preparation had been made, as soon as the event took place there was action from our world immediately. One cannot involve themselves in a situation such as the one we speak of. I apologise because at this time there is much confusion taking place. I am showing to Blossom that there is an angel of Light that is descending into the rubble, the aftermath. Many souls will not have passed to our world in fear, because of the preparation I spoke of. They will have been guided and given a helping hand. It is now, that the work must be done for many souls that have come to us. (It is difficult to keep our unity at this time. I speak of myself and Blossom, because of the disruption within the energies which affect all things). It is that certain souls chose to come with us because they did not have the strength to deal with their living facilities after this had taken place.

My friends, I was concerned as to the possibilities of speaking with you today. I feel that it is too difficult. I am showing to Blossom that I am a long way away. In order to speak with you it is requiring unnecessary energies. Whereas at another time one would be able to communicate more freely. I am showing that from where I am, coming down to you, there is a density of smog. This is what is causing the difficulty. There is so much work to be done to clear this smog. May I tell you that when it has been removed there will be a brighter Light that shines from us to you and vice versa. It has caused friction. It shall require strength for all to remove this vast cloud. It will require understanding on a level that many souls cannot comprehend. Where your souls feel the desperation for your brothers, you can, as you are aware, give Light to them. My friends, it is only the Light that can do any good at all.

I am showing to Blossom a pebble being thrown in the water. The ripple affect from just one pebble can spread out so far. This is what your thoughts can do. They can have a knock on effect. If each soul that resided upon your Earth came into their understanding at this very hour, it could literally be as if the buildings were again standing upright. This time is not to be. The Love that is emanating from many souls to another is already lifting the vibrations.

May I say for the first time, it is a little inconvenient for me to speak with you. You know my Love is with you. I would like you all to understand your hearts in this matter. I know I can be with you stronger as the smoke clears. For now I must retreat.

We give thanks to the Divine Oneness for allowing this meeting to take place. We ask always that we may remain humble in order to serve and that we may continue to walk in the Light and the Love.

Send Love my friends, as I know you are doing. It shall be a blessing to all.

Adieu, my friends, Adieu.

CHAPTER 28

WHITE CLOUD: A warm welcome to you my giggly girls!

I am giving to Blossom the image of a beautiful oak tree. It stands very tall, its branches have the circumference of a vast planet. I show that where the sunshine can come down onto the trees, it would seem that it is only the outer branches that can receive the Light. All the little leaves and twigs that are in the middle of the bush would not appear to benefit in the same way. Of course my friends, if you look at a branch that has its stem from the main source, it does not matter whether one can feel the Light from the sun or whether one can feel the Light from the outer part of the branch that receives it from the sun and sends it flowing through to what one would imagine is in the shadows. If you were to look you would see that the leaves from the branches that grow from the middle of the tree are as lushly green as the ones that are on the outer part. Just because you cannot always see what lies within the middle does not mean that it is not full of Light. I show that from this great oak tree there are little acorns. When they are ready to leave their nest, when they are mature enough to break the bond from whence they came, they fall gently onto the fields of grass.

I show that, rather than what you thought I was to say that the acorn would reseed into a new tree, that these acorns are picked up and taken to a home. They look very pretty, perhaps being placed in a bowl for decoration. By themselves they do not achieve their fullness. If you were to gather other species of nature, cones and leaves that have also decided to leave their roots, you could spray them with glitter, you could put false fruits into the bowl with these acorns. Suddenly they make the most beautiful oil painting. It is my friends, that although a single thing is beautiful for what it is, if it is prepared to share its beauty with others, the affect can be so much more when each individual thing becomes united to make the better picture.

I show that in time it maybe that perhaps some of the leaves or the cones, or whatever one has decided to join with, that they begin to dry and lose their freshness. It is then that those that no longer belong there should be removed. Although the picture is smaller it has a new affect. It has disregarded what once belonged there but after a time does not belong there any more.

I show now to Blossom and she is saying it is a bit early for all of this, I show a Christmas tree in the corner of the house. Throughout the year there maybe another item that resides in that corner or it maybe an empty space. Every year at a certain time, up goes that Christmas tree to bring the festive atmosphere into your home. Some choose to cover their tree with all sorts of paraphernalia, until you can hardly see the pines at all. Others prefer to have a few special bells hanging from the branches. What I say to you my friends is that it does not matter whether you pile on the decorations or whether you hang up just a few, ultimately the tree is still the same. How you choose to Light up this tree is your choice.

I show to Blossom that there are Lights upon this tree. It is one of those annoying things when one little bulb goes out. When you look you do not see all the pretty sparkling lights, your eyes are drawn to that one little bulb that has decided to play up a little. There comes a point when you must do something about it. It can be that you unplug the lights and by the time you get to the light that was out, you get confused, you have to go through the whole thing of trying each light. When you plug it in, because you paid so much attention to this little misdemeanour, it is that none of the lights work now.

It may be better not to focus on that little light that has gone out, allow it to disappear off the scene. Concentrate on the beauty of the other lights and how they shed their light onto the little baubles that are hanging close by. Perhaps the light that went out did so for a reason. Maybe the bauble that it once shone upon was no longer desirable to be noticed by the self. If you concentrate too much on such a little article, it can be that all the lights go out and you lose everything, instead of just letting go of that niggly tiny thing. Sometimes one becomes so frustrated trying to find which light is causing the problem, that after many hours of tedious frustration they throw it in the bin and go and buy a new set. This is appealing to the eye but then perhaps you might find that where that bulb was out, the bauble that was there trying to say to you 'no', is catching your eye too much. You need to remove that bauble because it is not pleasing to you. What I say to you my friends is that so often, one can go all around the houses until they realise what the message is. It is far easier to accept that that little light went out for a reason, that reason being not to bring attention to the bauble you did not like. You have wasted much of your energy by trying to replace it, thinking that that was what was required, when all the time, if you'd have asked what message this was trying to bring you, you would have heard in the first place that that bauble was trying to go.

Listen my friends to what your soul is trying to tell you. So many times you have a thought and you dismiss it because you start to doubt. You start to question instead of trusting that natural instinct. You usually find that after involving many other thoughts and possibilities that you come back in the circle to that original gut feeling. I am not saying it is wrong to look at other possibilities, I am saying that it is an advantage to you if you learn to trust what your soul is telling you in the first place.

I show to Blossom a clock upon the wall. The hands are spinning round and round and the hours are as if you have missed many of them. If you were to imagine watching that clock spin round, if you saw it, it would not be that you had missed it at all. You had been there to encounter it, it is just that it moves far more quickly now than you are used to. That is why, with this upliftment of the soul, it is important for you my friends, to make the most of every single moment however quick it is passing you by. I do not wish to be morbid, for I do not think of it in this way, there comes a time for all souls upon the Earth when they must leave their physical bodies and move on. Do not let it be that you move on having missed the best moments that could have been. You will not know whether or not you have, unless you assure yourself that you do make the best of each one. Then you can look back, you can say some were better than others, some were a thousand times better than others. Even the moments that did not feel so joyous were moments that you can live in, you can feel and know of. In all those moments learn my friends to feel your own Love. It is easy to feel the Love coming to you from another, it is an exhilarating sense of warmth. Learn to feel the Love that lives within yourself, then when your time to move on to another home comes, you cannot possibly regret one moment of Loving yourself. It is important we know to Love others. To Love yourself first is the importance of your time here.

My friends, do you hear the wind making music?

Wind chimes outside.

The wind always has a message to bring you. Listen to the wind. Listen to the rain. Listen to the clouds and the sun, for they all bring you wisdom if you care to listen to their voice.

We give thanks to the Divine Oneness for allowing this

meeting to take place. We ask always that we may remain humble and that we may continue to walk in the Light and the Love.

As always, my little chickens! it has been a pleasure to speak with you. I may have said this before, but I am old and my memory does not serve me so well!

KNOW WHO YOU ARE.

KNOW HOW FAR YOU HAVE COME INTO YOUR ENLIGHTENMENT.

Adieu, my friends, Adieu.

CHAPTER 29

WHITE CLOUD: A very warm welcome to you my friends.

I am showing to Blossom the image of a yacht that is on the horizon of the clear blue water. On the sail of this yacht there are thick red and white stripes and the No. 21. I show that behind this particular yacht there are many, many other yachts that are also in the race. It is as if, where the No. 21 yacht is ahead of the others suddenly the wind drops in that place and the yacht comes more or less to a standstill. All the other yachts with the wind behind them come sailing past No.21. Because they have been behind, the wind from there was able to carry them past, so they were not affected by the stillness of where No. 21 was sailing. It is, I show that No.21 is not concerned that the others are passing him by and that he now, from being in the position of the winner, is now at the back and could become the last one to finish. It does not matter to this little yacht because he is happy to be where the wind takes him. He allows the movement, the flow of the water to take him at the pace from where he is. It is even that the people upon this boat are so unconcerned regarding gaining the winning position, that they take the time to dive into the water and swim amongst the beauty of the creatures that lie within. When they have finished that part of their enjoyment they then come back to the boat and they make themselves some lunch. They are enjoying the moment. They are not concerned of how far ahead anybody else is. When they feel they have accomplished the pleasure that they could receive from that place in the water, with much relaxation and ease, they wind in the anchor and they are ready to move on with the breeze.

Ahead they can see that all the boats have crossed the finishing line. In their hearts they do not have competition with anyone else, they are happy to meander along until they reach the winning post that they are aiming for, but they are not concerned regarding the time it took them. When they arrive there they see all the other people from these boats. They are exuberant but they are exhausted because of the effort that had to be put in to being No.1. I remove the 2 from 21 because in my books No 21 is No.1 - the winner who came out on top. I show that when the others are celebrating their place in the race, quietly the people from No. 21 get back in their boat and go back again to pick up more people and give them the same ride, to show them that wherever it is that the wind drops, in that place, look around and make the most of where it is that you are at that time. Do not be forever struggling to move on and move ahead. When you are always looking at the finishing line and determined to win you forget to look at the beautiful sights along the way. Allow yourselves, my friends, to flow with the tide. Enjoy every aspect that it is showing you.

I am showing to Blossom a pole that is in the water. It can evaluate what level the tide is at. It can be that when the tide is high, if your boat is anchored to that pole, you are still high, you are in the same place, but you are at a higher level. With the natural flow of nature, gradually the tide will recede and the water level goes down. What you must see my friends is, that boat is still in the same place, it is just at that time on a lower level. When you come to the lower level you can see things along the ground that you were not able to see when the tide was in. You have a different perspective on all your views. So when the level is down, do not feel that you are forever waiting for the tide to come back. Look around. You will see beautiful little crabs and all sorts of things that you could not see from higher up. It does not mean when you are low that your eyes become shut. Make the most of the time when you are low, look around to see what new sights you can bring to yourself. I can assure you, that when that time has taken place and you have gained from being at that lower level, then and only then will the moon have its pull to bring the water level up again.

I am showing to Blossom that where the boat is anchored to the pole, sometimes one has had enough of this particular vista. They have cast their nets into the sea for their sustenance many times within that place, it is necessary sometimes to untie yourself from that place. You may not be able to see where the next pole is that you can anchor your boat. It is refreshing sometimes to just allow yourself to be set free from that knot and allow the tide to drift your boat in the direction of freedom. I promise you, that when it is time for your boat to set anchor again, the pole that you should remain around for a time will come into your vision. It is that when you are able to tie your knot there, to cast your net, there is completely new food. Food that you have not yet tasted before. There is a new enthusiasm that comes into your being because of the freshness of the scene. You will also find that at this new place the water level also goes down. Again it is in a new place. A different time to view the things that are around you. Some days when you are happy to set sail again you are happy to go with the tide. I show to Blossom now there are other times when you are prepared to get out your 'speed boat' because you know exactly where it is you want to go. You want to get there quickly. That is fine. It is for you to remember that some journeys are necessary in a speed boat and some journeys are best when they have a sail and let the elements of the universe guide you to your next habitat.

I am showing to Blossom that a large fish is caught. It does not look a particularly attractive fish as it lays there on the slab. It is uninviting to the taste buds, but at the time perhaps it is all the food there is. I show that when the fish is cut open there is a beautiful jewel that the fish has swallowed. You never know what is in the inside unless you are prepared to take a look. I show that the remains of the fish are discarded. The jewel is kept close to the heart. Take only my friends what you can receive from the inside and disregard all that is on the outer.

The following extract was for a lady in the group that had recently separated from her husband. She has given her permission for this to be printed as, like me, she feels it maybe beneficial for others in this situation.

I show now the image of a lawn. On one side the grass is very dry and barren, it has had no sustenance, nobody has cared for it and the rains have not come. On the other side is lush green grass. I show, with your permission xxxx, that you are sitting on the edge of the division. You have chosen to sit in the lush green grass. You have nurtured that place and you choose to sit in what you have created. I show that where you sit on the edge your tears drop onto the place where there has been no water and gradually your green grass spreads and nurtures the barren land. Your tears as they fall cannot spread to the end of that space, but in the place where they have fallen not only has the grass grown but flowers have blossomed there also. Give your Love as far as you are able to give, but do not try to reach a place that is beyond your reach, because if you were to do so, there would only be little patches here and there, that were not even of their fullest growth from the water. They would not have the necessary food to make them full. It is too much for one person to cover that amount. Concentrate on where you can reach. Pour that Love into that space. Make that space full of flowers and accept that your tears cannot reach further than they can fall. You will in time be able to accept that where your garden is, is where the Love was needed. The barren place is for the rains or perhaps another to come and water their own garden. It is not up to you to take on so much. It is for another to fill their own space with Love.

I am showing now the image of a man with wooden bottles that you can juggle with. Sometimes when one is juggling with two and they have mastered that, they then try for a third. This, when it is accomplished is another personal feat. Then one gets a little too big headed and tries for a fourth. They are forever dropping these wooden bottles because that soul has taken on too much. It is far better to juggle with three and perform all sorts of tricks rather than the monotony of the same movement, than to try and take on board a fourth when one's concept is not yet ready to understand the workings of the simple movement. When one is totally 'au fait' with the tricks of the three then perhaps it is time to bring in something new, but not until you have mastered the workings of the stage before. It is like, I show, when very gifted souls can put a spike on their heads with plates balancing and spinning on the top. It is that through practise this soul can manage to spin many, many plates. I show now there is the change to where the spikes are all in a row with plates going round. That soul who works those plates has spent a long time understanding what amount of pressure is required to allow the plate to spin as if it is not moving. It takes but one slip of the finger to bring a plate completely off balance. It wobbles and wobbles and you wonder if it shall fall. Once that has occurred then one has to concentrate on that plate with the different technique to gradually coax it. To give it care and thought to get it back on to this balanced level. At the same time the eyes have to be everywhere to think about the others that must still keep spinning around. It is like sometimes, the lives of the souls that live upon the Earth. Sometimes it feels that you have so many things to juggle around and keep in balance. It is that once one thing begins to wobble a little bit, you put your concentration into that and suddenly everything seems to be coming off its level.

I show to Blossom that sometimes it is too much pressure to keep them all spinning and level with each other. It is wise sometimes to take a step back and prepare yourself for the noise and let each plate smash to the floor. Simply get a dustpan and brush, sweep it up and put it in the bin. Instead of new plates on those spikes I place a little daisy on each one. You can watch them grow. There is no effort involved other than sending them your Love. It is far more pleasurable to pour water, which is your Love, onto a flower, at your own pace, than rush around trying to keep all these plates balanced. At the end of the show you can still step aside and take your bow because the audience can see beauty rather than you rushing around trying to perfect your balancing act.

I show now, and I am swapping and changing, the image of a piano. I show that there is one particular note that has been played a lot. The ivory has worn away. Amongst all these notes, this one particular note that has been overplayed gets stuck when you go to press it down. There is no longer the same tone that comes from it. The hammer inside those workings has worn thin so you hear the note but then it stops resounding. It no longer spreads its tune for others to hear. It can be that you can purchase certain waxes and so on to loosen this note, but eventually however hard and whatever you use to make something that is worn out back to how it was, it will never come to look the same even though it might have a little more grease to move it up and down. There comes a time when one will look at this piano and think that it is time to replace that note. When it is replaced, I show that it still sticks out because it looks so new against the others. With a little tender playing of that note it can blend in and become the same sound so that when all the notes are played you cannot tell that that particular note is a new one.

Is there a question at all before I go? I thought I would ask anyway!

May I ask a question White Cloud?

You certainly can and go to the top of the class!

When I am in a state of indecision how do I know which way to go?

I show to Blossom a shopping trolley at the top of two aisles. Both aisles are filled either side with many items. One is not always sure what one fancies for tea. One may spend a long time looking at all the items to see whether or not that something appeals to them for their supper. You can get to the end of the aisle and nothing has jumped out at you. You can turn round and come all the way back again down the other aisles and still there is nothing that feels right for you to eat. It is best then to leave your trolley and walk away. Purely by chance when you are wondering why there was nothing in those two aisles, why you did not find anything that could be good for you to eat, you are walking past a shop. You pass a fish shop and suddenly you know you would like some fish for tea. It is not always my friends when you are looking for your answer that you will find it. It is often when you allow yourself to just be, that the answer you are seeking will come to you as clear as daylight. You could have wasted many hours going up and down all the other aisles. You were looking for the answer to come. You were looking too hard. When you stop searching for the answer in your soul you allow the peace to settle. When you are calm amongst your own energies it will be the right time for the answer to come in and blend as a new energy. All the time you are up one aisle and down another, if the answer was to come in then, you would miss it because you were too busy looking elsewhere. It is hard at times to bring peace to ones being when ones mind is like a game of scrabble. You cannot find the words to place which will connect with another. Throw your scrabble board away and take up knitting my friends. Allow the calm to come to you, then surely as black is white! the answer will very shortly follow.

It is lovely my friends to have a small coffee morning today. Sometimes one needs the intimacy of a small group. That is the space that they feel comfortable in at that time. Other times one has the energy and the spirit to mingle amongst many. Always put yourself in the space that your self is asking you to be. Then all will be as should be.

We give thanks to the Divine Oneness for allowing this meeting to take place. We ask always that we may remain humble in order to serve and that we may continue to walk in the Light and the Love.

Go joyfully my friends in your beautiful blue skies. Until we speak again I bid you

Adieu, Adieu, my friends.

CHAPTER 30

WHITE CLOUD: Welcome to you my little bunch!

I am showing to Blossom the image of a white bird that is perched upon the olive tree. It has in its mouth the stem of an olive. I show that it takes flight. It comes to another land. It places this olive into the barren sand. I show then, that immediately roots are planted under the sand. They spread far and wide in all directions. It is the olive branch of peace my friends. It is a necessity at this time for your peaceful thoughts to spread far and wide. Until there is peace in all places upon your Earth it will not be possible for harmony and unity to endure throughout.

Again I ask you to realise the value of what your thoughts can produce. You may feel that 'just little me cannot do much,' But if every 'little me' gave their thoughts to places that require peace, it is natural law that the peace will come upon that place. I ask you first to recognise peace within yourselves, for how can you project peace if you do not fully understand its feeling. In this world in which you reside, because of your choice, it is very difficult at times to find that peace within yourself due to outside distractions. You can keep within your peace if you allow yourself not to be distracted by the outer part that is of confusion. When a soul from your world passes on to the next, one has the expression - 'They are at peace now,' this may not necessarily be the case my friends. If they were not at peace when they left, they still have to find the peace when they get there. You cannot go to a place called 'Peace', buy it and therefore have it. You must find your peace. There is no place called 'Peace'. There is a place within yourself that can become peace. When one is within this for themselves there is nothing and nobody that can intrude into that place. There is nothing that you allow to rile you, it is a fine place to be. The more that you dwell in that place the more you can give peace to others that you meet.

It is what you might call your disposition - I am re-tracking to say that it is a 'position' and what a nice position to be in. Ask for peace to come to you so that you can send it to others. Sitting in this room we are at peace, there is stillness and there is quiet. There are my friends, souls in other places whose eardrums have been broken due to the sound of bombing and gunfire. How can a soul when trying so hard to understand what is happening in their place of residence, how can they switch off and hear the silence? There are many souls that are working so hard to find peace within themselves in those countries, but all around is bloodshed and sorrow. It is a very advanced soul that can reside in such a place and be at peace with itself and its surroundings. Appreciate a little more where you are and where you have chosen to be. Bring in all that you can to you. The energies that are within your space are far easier to penetrate than for a soul that is amongst fire, as if they did not have enough to contend with.

I show to Blossom now a bird of a different type. If you were to look at these little birds in a picture book for a child, sometimes it would show that with the beak open there are musical notes that are coming out of their mouths. Listen to the music that these little birds bring to you. Be uplifted by their arias. Feel the liveliness in their soul. Allow it to penetrate your true self. Listen to their music with your spiritual ears and you can understand the message that they bring. Then too, you can learn to fly high with your own wings and sing your own song.

I show to Blossom now something completely different. I am showing to her a big red double-decker bus that they have in the land that she has moved from. Some people, when they get on this bus, feel that they only have a short journey to go, so why bother to go all the way upstairs because they will not be there for long. So they sit on the bottom deck and they only get the view from that level. They are limiting themselves because they cannot be bothered to make those few extra steps to the top. If they did, they could sit at the front and they would get a much greater perspective of their journey. Sometimes ones persona has the attitude on a particular day, due to the vibrations of the weather or your ladies hormones!, that you cannot have the enthusiasm to walk those few extra steps, perhaps another day when you are feeling more energetic. Always try, my friends, to make that little bit more of an effort, to push yourself a little bit. I am not asking you to climb the Eiffel tower, it is just a few steps to gain a better view. Also you would find probably, that the souls on the top deck are more interesting to talk to. They have made themselves use that little bit more energy to achieve something a little higher. For those that find it no effort at all to climb the steps, then they have a lot of energy left over anyway to pass on to you.

I am showing now that there is a bench by the bus stop. There is an older lady sitting there with her shopping bag waiting for the bus to take her home. As usual, especially in the country of England, one waits for a bus for a long time and then three turn up at once. For this lady, I show that having waited, being tired and needing to get home, that when the three buses come they are all going to her place but they take different routes. She is confused as to which bus she should get on. I am showing that it is for her to look at these three buses and to let her soul, which some people would call instinct, explain to her which one would be right at that time. It doesn't matter that one may take a longer route. One may go through a place that would be full of traffic. One would go through the country lanes. It matters that she takes the one that is instantly asking her to get on board, that is the journey that she is meant to take. She may prefer, because she is tired, to get on the bus that goes via the country lanes. It maybe, unbeknown to her that that bus will have a flat tyre along the way. Listen to what your soul is telling you. Do not put into question other things. Once you do that you allow your brain to become full of nonsense. These other questions do not need to be there. You have your answer and your direct knowledge by what you call your 'gut instinct.' That is your soul telling you what is right for you at that time. If you go against that and you get on the bus that has the flat tyre, it does not matter, it just means that you are bringing to yourself unnecessary confusion. You can learn from this confusion. You can learn that you should have taken the other bus. The feelings that your soul tells you are your book of wisdom and knowledge, it is all there written inside of you. Sometimes you may need to look up a certain chapter again just to confirm the strength within that feeling. Other times you can open the book and read four chapters in a row because it just flows so easily. Know that book is always inside of you. You can refer to its pages at any time.

I am now showing to Blossom the image of a bowling alley. One, when they are playing the game, has every desire when they let that the ball go, to knock down all of the ten pins. Sometimes when it leaves the fingers the ball can go a little off course and it knocks down only one. You wonder why? your thought and intent was to clear the deck. It is sometimes that your thoughts and your actions are a little out of sync to get the desired affect. It is necessary to repeat the same action, so that by putting in the practice one can build up the energy of determination required for that result. There can be other times, and this is to give you something to think about, that when you are playing the game and chatting to your friends, it just happens to be your go, your mind is not focussed on the end result so you just throw it anyway because it is a game. Low and behold it is a strike. What I am trying to say to you is that one can put too much energy into their goal. Sometimes it is better to just let it go, then you find that without even trying you can achieve the exact result.

I realise that within that little story there are many aspects to look at. On the one hand I say you may need to practice more and on the other I say to let it go. It is depending upon where you are at that time. It is wise sometimes to put in more effort if you feel it is necessary and requires that little bit more concentration. Other times it is wise to simply let it be. It is up to you to understand within yourself which of those ways of directing the ball is appropriate. You will find also sometimes that the minute you thought you had got what you wanted another ten come down!

There will always be more for you to achieve, always and forever. So I say enjoy playing your game of bowling. It is all a game after all so why make it have pressure. Enjoy it all, my friends, because that is why it has been placed in front of you. As I have said many times, Love it all. If you see something that is not of your instinctive liking, send it Love and then walk away. Do not walk away without giving anything your Love first. When you do, you might find that you might like to stay for a cup of tea. It is amazing how Love can change everything.

Now then class. Is there a question for me?

A friend of mine mentioned about prophesies made that the world would completely end by 2008. When you have small children, thinking that they have so much to live for and for yourself, I don't know what to think.

May I say to you with all respect, do not take what somebody else has written or spoken of so deeply as a Truth. It is your Truth that matters. If you sit at home and think 'will this world end in 2008?' then the negativity that that may encompass within yourself, may mean that in someway your world will end in 2008. I do not mean that you will pass on. It is my friend that nothing within the soul self can end. If in 2008, or 2013, or 2050, your planet was to disintegrate for example, your world would not be ended, your child's world would not be over, because you would simply have moved house to somewhere else. If you recall there were many prophecies that the world, so called, would end at the millennium. Are we not still sitting here upon that world?. Who is to say that this world is going to end at all? Maybe it will all merge into one. Try my little one, to be at peace. When all these things come into your earshot, be at peace. If it is going to end in 2008 there is not a lot you can do about it. Make the most of everyday until it happens. There are many things that people hear, it comes into their awareness, that one would care to ponder upon a little. If that pondering makes you feel sad and confused and in a bleak place, stop pondering about it. Look up at the sunshine. Go and see the beautiful blue sea. Fill your thoughts with what you have. Dispel confusion of what might be. Nobody knows what might be. You can only know 'what is'. Bring that sunshine into your being. Allow those Golden Rays to surround your soul, in that way little energies of confusion will find it very difficult to penetrate through. When you stand in your own strength you cannot have a bowling ball come and knock you down. I hope this has helped you in some way.

Is there another question at all?

Yes White Cloud I have another question.

My Goodness me! What has happened to you all?

My friend and I were discussing 'dimensions' last night. I wonder if you would be able to tell us what dimension YOU come from.

Straight away I gave to Blossom a number. Because she knows little of this, she is questioning me! She will trust and I can say that I reside most of my time, where my place is in Truth, upon the Seventh Dimension. It is my choice to come down to other places. It is, you may say, my holiday home.

Any more questions?

May I ask a question White Cloud?

You may always.

Thank you. Now that we understand the number of the dimension that your soul resides in, when you and Blossom partake together in the healing, do the healing energies come from your soul dimension through to the beings you are helping here.

As you know my friends, there are many aspects towards healing as to whether a soul should receive total healing, or minimal to help them a little, so therefore they come back for more and learn more. Also it is, with no offense to my friend Blossom, that the energies can only be of a certain vibration. I am showing an image of Blossom being blown flat against the wall. There is only a certain amount of power that can come through the human flesh. You may find this a contradiction in that, if this is a healing energy how could it damage Blossom? It has to be within a vibration that does not interfere permanently with the soul that is healing. I am with Blossom in healing, I am her teacher, so it is that Blossom is using her own healing energy although it is of one.

There have been times that Blossom is aware of, and for healers as we all are, that the dis-ease can disappear, if not instantly, but the next day when the energies have had time to disperse. This is not from my power, it is from the power of the soul that is being healed. It is merely a question of activating their own healing energy. If a soul needs to learn a few more lessons for itself, then the healing will not take place immediately. There is reason in all things, sometimes it is a matter of dealing with the issue that is causing the dis-ease. Until that is done there would be little point in healing the ailment, it would simply keep returning. One cannot escape the self my friends. If one can work towards achieving harmony within, then harmony can reside without.

My friends, the time has come once again to take my leave.

We give thanks to the Divine Oneness for allowing this meeting to take place. We ask always that we may remain humble in order to serve and that we may continue to walk in the Light and the Love.

Adieu, my friends, Adieu.

CHAPTER 31

Before this particular meeting began one of the lady's was asked to press the record button on the tape recorder once White Cloud was ready to begin speaking. She became all of a dither! We were having a giggle about it.

WHITE CLOUD: A warm welcome to you my friends.

I put Blossom off her stride just for a minute because I wanted to say well done to xxxx! You know we could continue on that note for a moment. Sometimes when there is a particular thing that needs to be done, because one maybe feeling a little apprehensive regarding this matter, they trigger off all sorts of confusions to their energies, because of a tiny lack of confidence that then grows and grows. It is, with no offense, a simple thing to press a red button. Sometimes one feels 'Will I get it right? Can I do this?' You know your finger can press a red button down. You allow fears and doubts to come in, which then races the heart and all sorts of movement begins to take place because of the signals given to the body. It is at these times my friends, if you feel anxiety regarding any matter, sit yourself down, recognise your Truth, know that these are simple things that have become out of proportion because of the place that you find yourself in at that time. There are other times when one is feeling full of joy and honour for oneself, that the same situation would not cause the anxiousness. Yet on another day one may be feeling a little out of sorts with oneself and the same matter becomes almost a mammoth task which produces sweat to the body and confusion in the mind. With all things, do not ask yourself 'Can I really do this?' - of course you can! You can do ANYTHING when you KNOW that it can be done. It is only your mind that allows you to hear otherwise.

I am showing to Blossom an image of her sweeping the petals away in her garden. She does this regularly, it is a task which is repetitive. Without a doubt, the next day the petals will be back again. It is for Blossom a sense of keeping things in place and making all around her neat and tidy. It is then one must do this within your thoughts. If your thoughts are messy and all over the place and out of order, how can one feel in order with the self? It would be advisable perhaps to give one a writing stick and paper and put all thoughts at random upon this piece of paper. In that way you can view them and begin to prioritise as to which thought should be No.1, No.2 etc. When you have all your thoughts in an organised fashion it is far easier to live out your day. Sometimes you wonder why you are feeling a little down, not quite yourself. On those days you feel lethargic. So you sit and thoughts churn over and over in your head. If these thoughts are allowed to just keep going over in the same rotation and one does not put them into a place, then the energy is going to be continually drained from you. Take the time my friends, to place your thoughts in a place that is of settlement. You will find that when you do that, there are some thoughts that cannot find a place. When they cannot, then you can become aware that they obviously do not belong there, so release them. Remove them from all that confusion that you have created. Discover which of these thoughts are useful to you. Keep them in there so that you can tap into them at any given time and KNOW that they are productive. Thoughts that confuse and pull on yourself will continue to do so unless you recognise that they are unnecessary

I am showing to Blossom now an image of a book that one would have at school, it has numbers and figures in. Children from an early age learn to add up numbers. Sometimes a child may miscalculate and the figure is wrong on the answer. It is that if one digit is missing, perhaps the answer should be nine and eight is put down. Blossom is surprised at what I say in that, in the bigger scheme of things perhaps it was meant to be that that one is missing. You have a saying 'It doesn't add up. It doesn't make sense'.

Communication was becoming very difficult at this point and I could not quite grasp his intention, which I need to do in order for his words to flow with ease.

Blossom is saying to me 'Do not lose the plot now!'.

It is perhaps that to one pers,hers say is fact. Fact can change. Truth can not.
Lets get off that subject as Blossom is getting confused, which takes us back to where we began!

Sometimes I find it very difficult to keep the train of thought going and start to doubt myself. I, at this point felt like calling the meeting to an end. The only way to describe it is, my brain really hurt!

I would like to say something. Blossom at this time is wanting to give up and I am asking if I can stay. I wonder what it is that I could say...

His voice became very emotional. I was taken by surprise when listening to the next part of the tape as I had forgotten this incident. Long pause. Very long pause! ...Then I hear myself burst into very dramatic tears! OOPS!

And on... and on... After many a shoulder there for me to cry on, discussions about how difficult I found it to do 'channelling' sometimes, and general 'That's enough about me. You talk about me for a while' indulgence. I felt that White Cloud needed to come back 'in' and speak. So I picked myself up, dusted myself down... etc etc.

I thank you for allowing me to continue.

I am showing to Blossom a basket of sweets. They are of the kind that when it is put in the mouth, one can choose to bite it straight away into little pieces - the result being that it does not last so long, or one can choose to suck on it to see how long it will last. Of course in that way, all the time it is becoming reduced, it is taking more time than if you crunched it. Either way one is still receiving the sweet but in the way that they choose to have it digested. Not only that, they also had to first of all choose the colour of the sweet, for they were all in cellophane so that the colour maybe viewed. One would think that choosing the colour of the sweet would have no thought at all. If you look, you must decide which colour you fancy at that time, you then unwrap it, then choose the way you take it in. A child still does this process. Their little way of being does not involve the deeper intuition. Once that sweet is inside the digestive system, again depending on how it was devoured, the body must react in a different way depending on little bits or just the juice that is left. When you take this sweet you do not say to your body 'Which would you prefer to digest? What way would you prefer today?'. You do what you do and what takes place afterwards happens automatically because of the way you have performed that action.

I am showing to Blossom now that in the same basket of sweets there is a large bar of chocolate. Why it is in there nobody knows, it is very distinctive from the other sweets. You then not only have the choice of which colour sweet you have, but there in front of you is another option. Your choice has become bigger. Because the chocolate stands out more, does this necessarily mean that that is the one you should take because it happens to catch your eye, because of its size. One would think that the choice would be the chocolate. Stop for a minute, recognise what you are looking at. It stands out more than the others, but it does not mean necessarily that it is the one for you. Look at the sweets. The chocolate is still in your vision but concentrate on the little things, the little sweets. When you decide to block out that chocolate and look and think of the juices that come into your mouth, you then KNOW because your heart is telling you, that one of these sweets would be far more desirable. It is that sometimes something big and strong comes right up to your face. It is as if you feel that this is what must take place. It is there in front of you and therefore it is for you to recognise and accept. This may not be the case, just because something is presented to you so strongly does not mean you have to go with that thing. I show to Blossom a gigantic bar of chocolate. Look either side because you do not know what is hiding round the back. Before you take action, check and double check with your heart that that is what your heart is asking you for. People say 'One thinks with the heart not with your head'. I say 'Always think with your heart' - once you allow your head to think you are starting a whole new book, full of confusions.

Listen to your heart. If that bar of chocolate is saying 'Eat me, eat me,' you think 'I do like chocolate but do I want that much?' When there is a little question regarding an action to take, just go round and have a little look further ahead. It may be that the chocolate was put there for a purpose, in order for you to recognise that you do not, anymore, feel the need to take that in.

I show to Blossom sparkly dust. In order for things to move they must be disturbed first. It is not possible for things to just come up in the same way from where they were. When anything rises there is movement. If you imagine all your sparkle is being shifted and getting muddled and entwined in order to get up to that next level - be patient my friends, because if you think, in order for it to settle on that level, first of all it must go a little higher in order to come down and lay its place. So whilst it is up and ready to come down, you are in a place that is too much for you to be in, so again I say, allow 'all' just to be. Wait patiently KNOWING that at this particular time the stardust is gently falling and once it has settled all shall be in balance again.

I am in a little bit of a pickle because there are things I wish to say but Blossom can already feel that she could not manage to say these things because of emotion. I suppose I can learn my lesson too today and trust that what I would like to say, I do not have to show her a picture of, because she can just feel my Truth. What I would say though is what we have spoken of before - when one is taking grades in a particular subject one practices and works hard in order to pass Grade 1. They feel elated that they have achieved something, until they go for their first lesson for Grade 2. All of a sudden they feel they know nothing. With work and with practice the confidence builds and they fly high in passing Grade 2. So it continues up the scale. This is what is happening to Blossom. She has passed certain Grades. Now, as with all subjects, the higher your grade becomes, the deeper and the more there is to uncover.

She is saying to me 'Thank goodness for that!'.

It is merely, my friends, a question of putting your thoughts in order. May I say, you need to understand your thoughts. Blossom did not understand what was happening, now that I have explained, that thought can settle there and be accepted. If you do not understand your thoughts how can you ever be at one with them?

Before I go, I just handed to Blossom, she saw me give her a red round lollipop. She asked what this was. The lollipop turned into a... in the country she comes from they call it a 'Rosette'. I am giving her, her first prize. She has earned it.

His voice was very emotional and the Love that he sends through to me is overwhelming sometimes. This was one such occasion!

We give thanks to the Divine Oneness for allowing this meeting to take place. We ask always that we may remain humble in order to serve and that we may continue to serve in the Light and the Love.

Adieu, my friends, Adieu.

CHAPTER 32

WHITE CLOUD: A warm welcome to you my special friends.

I am giving to Blossom the image of what you call a pincushion. It has many pins that are placed through to the core. If a particular pin is required for its purpose, then it is removed from the place where it was last set. When it has done what it came to do, then it is very unlikely that the pin will be put back in the same place. It maybe that as the pin is pushed into this cushion that the stuffing inside has a little knot where the pin is to be replaced, so it will not go in as deeply as you may require. Now out of determination, one can either keep pushing away at that pin and have a struggle and become agitated, or one can leave it at that place as far in as it will go this time, or they can remove it and put it in a place where it goes in smoothly and much deeper. It would depend you see, on where the soul, who is placing that pin, is at that particular time of that day. I show to Blossom now that there are rows of pins. They are not just put anywhere in random order. Upon this particular cushion they are lined up equally in a row and then below that is another line, but not so many and then a line underneath, so that it is taking the shape of a triangle you understand. When one views this pincushion in this way, if that was to feel in order and comfortable with the eyes that are viewing it, it can be left alone. I show that there is a pin taken from the bottom row and it is placed above the very top row of the pins. Then one tends to think 'Well, I can experiment a little now because my creativity has suddenly come into being and I can have a little play with this', so you take another pin and put it above the first level. Before you know it, you have completely recreated the pattern that was there. You find that all the pins that were at the bottom have been moved up to the higher level. Then, if you like, you could take the next row from the bottom and place them above the ones you have already put at the top. What I am saying to Blossom is that it is not always necessary for you to go through each level step by step. Blossom is surprised at this because this is what she always thought, that you must work your way through. Sometimes it can be that you stayed at the bottom for a certain time and then you can, when you are ready to be moved, make a gigantic leap ahead of the other pins that you thought were far higher than you were. It can be done in this way, depending on knowledge from times before. It maybe that you were ready to stay at the bottom level for quite a time, you were eager for somebody to pick you up and just move you one level ahead, but no! you stayed at the bottom. By staying there you are able to accumulate and prepare yourself for that leap.

I return to the stuffing that is in the middle of the pin cushion... Sometimes there are patches that can get a little clogged up. It is that every now and then you might give the cushion a little shake to even it out a little because it is looking a little lumpy somewhere and a little thin somewhere else. I would ask, that why would one take a pin and think about putting it in one of the more lumpier places? That is what one's tendency tends to do! - it is obvious that there is a thicker clump to get through but it looks like it is a place that has enough sponge to see it through. You know really that there must be a lot of knots there, it is better, rather than just to have a stab in the dark, to look at the cushion. Have a little feel as to what feels soft and what does not, then gently place your pin into the softer part. If you choose to keep pushing it through the hard knotty bit, eventually you will get through. Why go to all that extra effort when right next door is a softer place.

It is also that one tends to shake up the cushion to change its lumpiness because you think that is the way to do it. Perhaps it might be more soothing to put your hand against this lump and caringly smooth it down, in that way it becomes flatter and smoother and evenly spread, compared to the fact that when you shake it, all it does is move that lump from over there to over here. Look at the different ways that could be, when you know that there is something that needs ironing out. The way that your indoctrination has taught you is not always the simplest way around things.

I would like to speak regarding indoctrination. My friends that are here are aware of the Truth. You know, within this marvellous miracle that sits inside your head, there are many, many things that it chooses to hold on to. It is only when one becomes deeper and deeper into their Truth's soul, that they can disperse of past feed through. Even when one knows that certain things they were taught are not their Truth, it is that this other teaching can sometimes remain inside. Although your true self believes it has let it go. I show to Blossom an image in the head of two sections, one is labelled 'Truth for me', the other is a hole. I show that with a spade, the hole is being filled up with all the knowledge that is not beneficial for you. It is good to visualise taking that pile into a bin sack, putting it all in and tying it up. Visualise taking it out of here and dispersing with it how you may. It is of quite a degree of importance that you actually give yourself the time to remove this. It is like a computer that you have. You may have a document that you no longer need so you delete it, it goes to the recycle bin. If you want to have that back, you can. If you do not want it back, it is still there somewhere. It is therefore part of everything that is inside the computer. It is mingling with all other components, even though when you bring your screen up it no longer shows that it is there in the forefront. It is a wise thing to not only remove indoctrinations, remove all thoughts that no longer belong inside of you.

I show to Blossom now an image of something completely different. I show her an image of a red ice-lolly. It is that it is recently out of the freezer. It has little white spots of ice still upon it. One would think that when they put it in their mouth it was for the purpose of relieving the thirst, instead, they put it to the mouth and the ice sticks to the lips! Sometimes you look at something that you want immediately because you are so thirsty. It is sometimes wise just to be patient and wait that little bit longer for something you really desire. By putting it in the mouth with the ice sticking, all you get is pain, but you wanted it then. If you just wait, the juices have melted a little. When it is time for that thing that is ripe to come to you it shall.

We often feel and I have heard you say that you are ready for this thing that you desire. Perhaps 'you' are, but perhaps 'it' is not. Do not think that it is you that is preventing this coming to you. Perhaps, whatever it is, needs to come into its full maturity. Then you can reap the full benefits. So my friends, when you are feeling a little impatient, think about that ice-lolly. If you just wait until it is correctly aligned in all things, then when it does come, you will be so glad that you did not get it before.

I have asked Blossom if it may be that I may, as this is our last group for a time, if it is alright for me to touch your souls via these instruments? *(eyes)*.

Of course, my Blossom never turns me down!

Much deep breathing and patience.

I have just shown to Blossom that which I would like to achieve. Already her eyes bring that water!
I am going to stand. There is no need for hustle and bustle for I am in my strength.

He, (me), did so. He went round to each person in the room and made direct contact with their eyes - the windows to your soul. Individually he wished everyone a 'Happy Christmas' as he did so. All very moving. His Love makes many dissolve in to tears.

Unfortunately I do not have any money to buy you presents. Accept what I have given you today with a heart that is ever expanding because of you.

We give thanks to the Divine Oneness for allowing these wonders of Light to be upon us. We ask always that we may remain humble in order to serve and that we may continue to walk in the Light and the Love.

Ho! Ho! Ho!, my friends to you. I imagine I would rather suit one of those red outfits with my tummy. My friends... I Love you.

Adieu, my friends, Adieu.

CHAPTER 33

WHITE CLOUD: A warm welcome to you my friends.

I am giving to Blossom the image of a fire that is in the centre of a gathering. The flames are of the purest colours, reds, oranges and gold. I am letting Blossom hear the crackling of the sticks as they warm. It is that the fire reaches its fullest capacity and the glow that it sheds all around is of magnificent beauty. It is that if one were to be present in this place their hearts would be as warm as their faces. As the sparks of Light rise up into the night sky, then ones hopes, dreams and thoughts are also taken upwards with the flames to be put out to the Oneness. When it is time for the fire to finish, it is for a while that there are just the embers that are glowing like hot coals. They also, when they have had their day, return to ashes.

When one looks into a fire that has taken place and is no more, it is hard to imagine that not so very long ago that same image that one sees now was alive, alight with brightness. When one looks when it is over, there is nothing to show of what once was. With all things my friends, there are the flames, the aliveness, the brightness, while that particular energy is allowing itself to be in its fullness. It is that when the time for all things to calm down and return to the source takes place, then it is very difficult to imagine the feeling, the experience, the emotion that one had whilst it was going on. When it is over, sometimes it is that ones soul can feel very flat, as if the cinders can be so easily blown away with the wind.

It is for you to know my dear friends, that when a particular circumstance is taking place, that is the reality of the now. It is for you to know that 'the now' will always remain with you, even though it will become what you call 'in your past'. If the Love energy is allowed to remain within your being, then it is that when the ashes are blown away, there is no feeling of regret or remorse. The entire experience has not blown away. It has remained within yourself. It is also, that where perhaps this ground is, that once the ashes have gone, it has burned that place on the ground. As many of you know, it is through the fire, the death from the fire, that can bring about new life. So allow those ashes to be blown. Know that it is leaving a space for new life to be born.

I am showing to Blossom now, a tree. It has a large branch and from this branch there has been made a swing, out of rope. It has a plank across for one to sit on. I show that at this time, there is no soul sitting upon this contraption. The wind is allowing it to sway freely back and forth. There is no weight upon it. It is free of all burdens and therefore able to move freely also. When the wind stops and the stillness comes, then perhaps the swing shall come to a standstill. It does not mean that it has lost its freedom. It means only that it is pausing for a time in the quietness and the stillness of itself. One cannot keep on moving continually without allowing the time of the stillness. To regain energy. To regain balance.

I show then that a soul is put upon the swing. The wind blows again. This time it is much harder for the movement to take place naturally. It is that the burden the swing now carries, must set about allowing the swing to move. What if perhaps the swing still wanted to be still? What if it was not yet ready to start its movement along its path at that time? What if another energy came along that forced this movement to take place, without the permission of that swing. I am letting Blossom hear that the rope is creaking as it moves back and forth under the weight it is carrying, under duress.

It is though, that sometimes throughout your lifetimes, that one may have to carry certain burdens, to help another soul get through a particular time of their lives. It may feel that you are creaking and groaning with the weight that you have taken on. If you can come from a place in your hearts my friends, of understanding that others burden, then you will not mind in taking that extra burden, for that time that they wish to swing along with you.

I know that in your world you have a song which is called 'He ain't heavy he's my brother.' When a soul that comes to you is in need of your Love, pick him up and put him on your shoulders. Carry him across the waters that he cannot cross by himself. He is afraid perhaps he might drown. By allowing him to go across above the level that would frighten him, then there is no fear. By making the very action of lifting him onto your being, it is that he could put his trust in you and all fear is removed. It maybe that you can't swim either! It is that when one is giving to another soul, fear is gone. You are not thinking about the concerns of yourself. You are only thinking of helping that other soul. You put all your doubts aside for that time. It is, when you get to the other side of the river, that you can place that soul down beside you. Together you can look back and you can laugh. You have accomplished such a feat together. Your strength has become as one. I show then to Blossom that there are two pathways. It is that you can go yours and that soul that you helped through such deep water is able to freely continue on his own pathway. I show also that as you are walking off and your friend has gone out of sight, feeling good about oneself, that you may hear a voice from afar. You look back and across the other side of the river is another soul asking to be brought across. There maybe turmoil in your soul. It takes a great deal more understanding than before to have to go all the way back again, to return to a place where you felt you may never have to go back to. What do you do? It is your choice my friends. I show that because of the Love within the heart, that one could not possibly ignore that plea for help. My friends, as one walks back towards the river I show that suddenly out of nowhere there is a boat with an engine upon it. You can go straight across and your souls that are in need can easily come straight across the river with you because you have done it many times before now. The way was made much easier because of he Love that you were prepared to give.

It is then that you can go on your journey. The boat is there so perhaps some of the souls that have been brought across may decide to stay, just to be in that place and wait for another to arrive on the other side so that they too can give their Love. You can then walk on to waters that are further ahead. It maybe that when you get to these waters that they look far too rough for you to cross. I am showing to Blossom lots of bubbles and current. You may feel after your long journey that you do not have the strength to make it across. That is when another Angel shall appear to you to do the same for you as you have done for another. That is natural law my friends.

Not so long ago I spoke to you regarding taking note of where you were in your own space at that time. Not many of your weeks have gone by so far, but could you honestly sit in this space now and say that not very much has changed? Blossom I know is using often the words 'It is the quickening'. All I can say is, if you think this is quick, then you had better put a rope around your waist and anchor yourselves down. There are times for all when confusion and doubts and fears, apprehension, negativity, all emotions must be present as well as the Love, the laughter, the Light, the joy, the warmth. You must, as you know, experience the opposites to know one from the other. So when the confusion and the doubts are at the forefront, accept them. Know that in a day or two the others shall take the lead in the race. It is part of the all. I say this if I may, those that walk the Earth with their feet upon the ground in flesh are what you call human beings. Do not ask yourselves to be angels and then be cross because you cannot live as an angel. If you were an angel you would not be walking in the flesh at this time. That is not to say that to me, each one of you are my angels. Although it is for the advancement of your soul to grow as you learn, do not condemn yourself as you are learning. That is all I have to say regarding that matter.

It is for me that Blossom can see the flame that is flickering behind her eyes although her eyes are shut. I am very happy that you thought of me regarding your fire.

We were going to have a bonfire and wondered if White Cloud would like to come through and open his eyes to experience this once again as he did in his last reincarnation on Earth.

It is for me, enough to see the flame of the candle flicker. To feel the warmth from your hearts touching my very soul. It is, as of the days around my own campfire, when the Love and understanding of matters that were of importance were shared by many hearts, but it is as if they were one. That brings a sweet memory to me. I give thanks that I am able to be in the presence of such dear friends.

We give thanks to the Divine Oneness for allowing this meeting to take place. We ask always that we may remain humble in order to serve and that we may continue to walk in the Light and the Love.

Walk your road with peace in your heart. If you feel perhaps that you do not have the strength to carry another across the river by yourself then buy yourself a rubber ring!

It would be a wonderful advancement for me if one day I could let you hear the sound of my laughter. It is only that I can make that noise like one of your animals with a wiggly tail. It is that when I laughed upon the Earth it was as if my tummy would shake. The depth of the vibration that came forth was as you would imagine your Santa Claus to be. How I Love to laugh. Laugh, laugh, laugh my friends because many things are funny. Make sure that you see the fun that is there for you to see. Do not walk with blinkers on missing all the fun that is either side, because sometimes the road ahead looks pretty bleak.

Take care of yourselves until we speak again. My Love is always with you.

Adieu, my friends, Adieu

CHAPTER 34

WHITE CLOUD: A warm welcome to you all.

I am showing to Blossom a bunch of bananas. On the outer layer of the skin there are quite a few speckles. The skin is being peeled off from the banana, so what is inside can be revealed. How white and pure the fruit is once the outer layers have been removed. It is the time now my friends that these outer layers that have been there since that banana was growing, it is time for them to come off. It is no longer fitting that the fruit inside is marred by the over ripe part of the skin. It is no longer necessary to be part of that fruit. If one does not begin to remove the skin in time, then it will infect what lies underneath. Remove from your beings all the layers and the little speckles that have been with you for too long so that the Truth that lies underneath the skin can be revealed.

I am showing now the image as I have once done before, of a light bulb. It is so necessary in these times to turn up the dimmer switch. Not a little at a time any more. Whack it up to full so that the Light can be seen from all angles and all around. I am aware that in your hearts you know of this. Without wishing to sound condescending, if you could see from where I am sitting, you would realise the importance of doing this now. We know in our hearts what must be done. I am aware that many souls upon your Earth spend much of their days fulfilling their tasks to bring souls to the Light. It is time to, may I say, work not just a little but a lot harder. Those who are able to spread their Light must realise now the importance of this time upon your Earth. There is so much work to be done. It can be done. It will be done. My friends, we need your assistance.

I am showing to Blossom in the skies as far as one can see,

armies, armies preparing for their duties. I am showing to Blossom underneath your soil, armies, armies preparing also for battle. I speak this night in a way that I have not before. I know that all of you know that my Love for you is as strong as Love can be. I say to you in bluntness, do not play at this game. The time is now. Do you not come across many people, who you are aware have no idea at all as to what lies ahead? I ask you my friends if it is not appropriate to use your language to them, plant the seed in their souls through your mind. The power that your mind has to reach to the energy of that soul can make all the difference. Find ways in the way that you speak with another to plant that seed, to find the right words that will make them wake up and ask you for more and more.

I will say to you, there are many souls that shall get left behind at this time. Try my friends, to make the number that remain as few as possible. To confuse the issue I would say, this is not for ever. It is for this time. There shall be other times. How long is time?

I feel that I have been rather, I choose the word, dogmatic. My heart is full of Love. It is necessary to express these words in the manner that I have because of the anxiety that is among us. The Light must be spread NOW! You may think that perhaps I am saying these words to the wrong people because you already know. The intensity of my words can help you understand just a little bit more of what is to take place.

I am showing to Blossom now on a lighter note the image of some children that are playing with a skipping rope. There is a child holding the handle one side and another child holding the other handle and they are spinning the rope. As it spins round and round, it is a question for the child who is to jump in to get the rhythm within it's being before it takes the chance to run in and jump with the flow of the turn. Feel the rhythm that is around you my friends. Allow yourself to become in rhythm with the energies that are so close to you. It shall be that when you are sure that you know the exact time to run in and take a jump, that you shall do so and find yourself as one with that rhythm. If one was to take a chance before they really understood what speed that rope was turning, because they were too eager to get in there, they would find often that immediately they ran in, they would trip and stand on the rope and it would stop. Then what would happen? They are out. They have to go to the back of the queue and wait all over again until once again their turn comes around. There are energies that are upon your Earth plane now that are around you, that are of a different type. Take the time to absorb them within your energy field. Take the time to listen to what they have to say. Take the time when you have listened to absorb and understand. There are messages my friends that are coming at a rapid pace for those who are willing to listen. Learn to allow your energy to enfold with these new energies. This requires as I always say, the time for you to sit and allow this to take place. As you learn to blend, then this is when you will eventually hear the messages that are coming. The messages will be profound. Some messages will shake you to the core, some messages will make you want to lie on the floor, look up at the sky and do nothing but smile. Be strong my warriors, follow always the Truth in your hearts.

I am showing to Blossom a Golden chalice. I ask of you that when your eyes become open in the new morning to visualise taking one sip from this chalice. Each day I ask of you to take another sip.

Before I go I am showing to Blossom that around this table there are paper cups and cakes and little sandwiches. There are balloons with ribbons coming down. I would not wish my dearest friends to leave you on a note of melancholy, therefore I show you this picture to let you know that it is also time for you to celebrate. Blossom can hear the noise of the party blowers. Spend each day as if it was a party. Feel the joy in your hearts. When there is a party in a house and people walk by, they hear the noise of the blowers blowing, balloons banging and clapping and merriment and mirth. What do you imagine they do? They smile. Their hearts are uplifted also. I do not doubt for one moment of your Love, your Truth, your Light and your determination. We are so very proud of you.

We give thanks to the Divine Oneness for allowing this meeting to take place. We ask always that we may remain humble in order to serve and that we may continue to walk in the Light and the Love.

There was a long pause. I could feel that White Cloud wanted to chant. He had wanted to many times before. To be honest I just was not sure about this! Anyhow, this particular time I decided to go with the flow. He chanted for a while. Everyone in the room felt the vibration of his tone. They said it touched their heart.

Adieu, my friends, Adieu.

CHAPTER 35

WHITE CLOUD: A warm welcome to you all.

I am saying to Blossom the song of 'Somewhere over the rainbow'. It is the myth that at the end of the rainbow is a pot of gold. If you look at a rainbow in the sky, the wonderment within your soul is enormous. Where all of a sudden do these beautiful rows of colours come from? Where do they start? Where do they end? The point my friends is that there IS a land that you dreamed of. The song goes on 'If happy little blue birds fly beyond the rainbow, why oh why can't I?' I feel you are all aware enough to know my friends that you can and you do.

The pot of gold is awaiting you there. Not in the form that is sketched in a children's book. It is for you to know that these colours are all around you, all of the time. Because one cannot see them prominently in view does not mean that they are not there. There is a reaction that takes place when the rain falls and the sun shines that causes this to be. There is a reaction that is inside of you that perhaps, when the rain falls but the sun shines, you are not able necessarily to see with your eyes these colours but you can feel them all around you. I show to Blossom a little chap that is known as a leprechaun. Where did this little chap emerge from? Is he an idea in somebody's head that has grown throughout your world? Or was it that quite a few people came across this leprechaun one-day and many others besides? I do not as I have said before, wish to teach my grandmothers how to suck eggs, but just because one has not experienced something does not mean it does not exist.

It maybe that two souls are together in the woods. One may see the nature spirits all around, the other may see nothing and therefore think the other that does, has gone a little loco! To the one who can see so clearly it is the other soul that is denying the Truth of what is there. That again leads me on to the fact that each one of you, to each soul, the Truth is different from another. Because the other soul cannot see these little beings, the Truth for them is that they are not there, for they are not, for they cannot be seen and that is the Truth. To the other it is a very different Truth. Who is to say which Truth is the Truth? In that sense one cannot pin point Truth. Truth my friends is your Love inside yourself.

If one soul believes that when they move to another place, that there is nothing. For a while until they can adjust, they will sleep and there shall be nothing, because that is what they have given to know for themselves. Another soul who knows that they have lived by their Love and their Truth, and that when they are fortunate enough to move into other realms, there will be a place of rainbows. When it is their time to take that journey they shall arrive in a place of rainbows. Neither one is wrong. They are simply abiding by their Truth.

I am showing to Blossom the image of a puddle that is from the rain that falls. Is it not so my friends that sometimes because of certain elements that are perhaps there before the puddle, that one can look into it and again the rainbow appears? The same colours that may even be caused by the leaking of the oil from your automobile. Even when the rain comes and the car breaks down there are still rainbows to be found. There shall be in days ahead, rainbows that you have not yet seen with your human eyes. Blossom is saying to me, 'is this a musical or what'? Because I am saying to her, 'look, look, look to the rainbow', find all that you require. If you were to set on a journey as we all do, we have no idea where or when that journey shall end. We keep on and we keep on. There is something that is pulling us to that place 'Way, up high.'

I am showing to Blossom the image of what she would make out to be an old fashioned wash board. It is her confusion as to whether it is a large cheese grater! On the one side there is the smoothness and on the other the jagged edges. I show that an article of clothing is being moved up and down on the smooth side. In this way the item cannot be torn or dishevelled. It is running smoothly. It takes but one flip to the other side and it could be that the clothes are ruined because of the coarseness of the board.

I show that the clothes are hanging upon the line. They have many tears upon them. I show that this article when dry is then put in the basket with all the other clothes that are acceptable to wear. It could be that this particular dress was one that a soul favoured. One of their comfortable outfits and they are loath to put it in the bin. It is in your mind, the thought that perhaps you can take a needle and patch up what needs to be repaired. I show that when this is done it does not look as it should. One realises that it can perhaps be used for a duster or it needs to go in the bin.

Sometimes my friends, when things that are around you or within you have been damaged, it is wise to try to make amends. Perhaps sometimes these things that you felt comfortable with and had favour towards, perhaps they became unrepairable for a good reason. To have that in your life as a patched up job would never be the same as the original form, therefore it is better to remove it totally from yourself. It maybe some days that you go to take that dress out of your cupboard and you remember that it is no longer with you. There maybe a few little pangs because that dress is missed by you. You have to find something to wear. You begin to look for other items that you feel comfortable wearing. Eventually that dress that you were so fond of is just a distant memory that does not touch your heart at all. It was not meant to remain with you. On the other hand there are some items that might get damaged, but instead of throwing them away, an inspiration comes to you as to what you could put on that little patch that is worn. You can repair something to give it an advantage more so than it had before. Sometimes when something becomes worn out, it does not need to be removed it just needs to be replenished to give it new life. There are many things within yourselves my friends, as I have said before, that one tends to leave dormant because they do not know within themselves how to wake it up. Sometimes one needs to go to that thing that is sleeping and give it a good shake. Unless that is done they will sleep for infinity. It is like a little child who wakes up grumpy sometimes. It is as if you do not want to wake them because you know what you are going to have to deal with when you do. Once that child has come out of its sleepiness and puts on a beautiful smile and gives you a kiss, it was well worth the effort of waking them. In the same way, a dowdy dress that you no longer wear, look at it again, see what you can do with it to make it become something you want to wear.

So much can be done because of the power that you have up here. *(Points to head.)* You are aware because your electrical boxes have told you, that only a very small percentage of your brain is used. This is very much also the same as the spiritual side of yourselves. You are daily working towards finding the whole. It can only come a bit at a time. There are some that choose not to use it at all. There are some that choose to use it in the wrong manner.

There are many who choose to use it for Love.

I would like to speak a little regarding the aspects that were spoken of last evening. If you are on a pathway and you are in the middle, if you look one way all you see is beautiful sunshine and blue skies. If you turn round to the other side, the clouds are forming and it looks very much like there shall be a storm. Which one would you decide to take? Walk to the

Light my friends! The rain clouds might come further up towards you. If you are walking, continually walking to the sun, if that sun is coming to you and you can feel its strength and its warmth, even if little drops of rain manage to reach you, the warmth that you have already received would dry that rain up instantly.

I am showing to Blossom that one is on the sunshiny side - 'The sunny side of the street.' if you like. I am showing as an example only, there are little children who are caught in the thunderstorm. They can see that if they run they shall get wet in the process but they can see that further down the line they can be in this Light. You are standing there dry as a bone. It is my friends, that some little children and adults, want with that deepest emotion to be dry again and live in the sun. It is they that you will see running towards you, trying to get to you. That is when you hold your arms out and you encourage them 'Come on, come on.' Sadly there will be many who will enjoy that rain, if I can use that word enjoy. They choose to live under the cloud. For them, they can be so far in that storm that it is for them, such a long way away, that the brightness does not do anything for their hearts.

I have said to you before, for what Blossom and I have chosen to do, if we can turn one head around then we have done our job well. You cannot turn everybody's heads if they do not want to look. You can send that Light to them. Some souls are so far down that rainy road that, in Truth my friends, the Light has dissolved before it can reach there, some souls are that deep in their mire. There are souls in my world and yours who are trained and there are many discussions held of tactics etc, in order for them to go to such a darkened place. It is also that with them must go a soul of high estate, it is necessary for their protection. It is not to say that all souls in that darker place choose to be rescued. They are familiar with their darkness. There is a greed with inside of them for that avarice to take over their whole being. They do not wish to have to work at themselves when they can have all that they want just like that. There are some souls that are touched and they are brought very slowly into the Summerland. Even then, a soul can be in the Summerland for a time, but if there is another soul connection with a soul that has chosen not to come, that pull can be so great that the soul returns again to the darkness. All that I am asking is not for you to concern yourselves with the troubles of the entire universes, I simply ask of you to give it your best shot. That is all you can do.

Sometimes, as I understand it, one may not be feeling in the right place within themselves to, in all Truth, want to be bothered. Do not knock yourselves about because you are not giving to another one hundred per cent of every minute of your day. When Love is within you, it is naturally being given out by you. Do not feel that you have to make such an effort all the time and get confused if you do not feel that way about a certain thing.

KNOW THAT YOU ARE LOVE.

When you know that is who you are, the job is already done. You do not have to do anything other than BE. Yes it is correct to send thoughts to those in need. Do you not see my friends, that when you are walking along your beaches and you feel as high as the kite flying in the air and everything around you is Love, do you not realise that you are giving out Love? That Love goes to those souls in need naturally. It is out there. It does not have to be this heaviness. Would you think that creation was made to always carry buckets of water upon your shoulders? Or would you think that creation was meant to have little butterflies that flap on your shoulders and cool you down. The fact of Lightening up is what we need to work upon! It is your laughter that brings souls to the Light. It is your smiles, your Light heartedness that brings souls to the

Light. Enjoy, enjoy, enjoy your life.

You came down to this plane to achieve certain goals. To expand your Light. Sometimes one must go under a little to be able to come out again and feel the Light. You have spoken recently that the man that was called Jesus upon this Earth plane has said the words 'I have suffered so you need not.' Even when there are dilemmas coming at you from every angle, it does not need to become so intense, if you trust and you know that it is all happening because it is happening. As you know, it is how you choose to approach that dilemma that makes it a Light dilemma or a heavy one.

I show now the song of 'With a knapsack on my back'. It is sometimes that one needs to gather together all the resources that are needed for the journey. They are neatly put on the back and off you go a wandering, with a whistle and a song because you are happy to be going along that track. There is no need for the knapsack. You already have all the resources you need inside of you.

Is there perhaps a question that I may advise you upon. Have you got your list my friends?

Yes. I have one. Just to clarify the concept of God. Christianity knows this as God the Father, and others believe that God the creator is a woman. Can you explain this concept a little more for me?

Just a little question then! I do not wish to show Blossom a picture on this. Blossom is not believing I am going to say this or is she hearing it right? What if Christianity chose to call God, 'The Knitting Needle?' What if they chose to call God, 'The Fish?' My friends, God to you is your God. For many, many years, it was God is 'He, The Father' then for certain times in days gone by and times now, God can be to some souls 'She, The Mother'. Who is to say? Who was the person that said 'God is The Father'? Who was the person that said 'No, it is The Mother!' It does not matter. If, as Blossom was brought up in the church of Catholicism, one is given the figure of a man that you call God, sitting up there with a long white beard in a white robe, looking down and pointing the finger. Therefore it is difficult when, from a child you have been indoctrinated with that image. For Blossom, not that long ago, to connect with the feminine energy of 'Oneness' was easier. It is not female or male, it is Love. There are male and female energies that exist. They are in your human form. You have the gender of a male or a female or a bit of both sometimes. Your soul is all or neither. It does not matter what you choose. It is not father, mother, son, daughter, it is Love. As you rise into the realms of Light that are so Divine, you will see that there is no, if you like, 'I fancy a bit of that!' - that does not exist anymore. For me personally, I choose to use the Divine Oneness as opposed to God The Father, that is my choice. Others choose to worship other symbols, other icons, that does not matter either because that icon is still part of the Oneness. If it is that, that is allowing that soul the freedom, I must stress, within that religion to do the work of the Oneness, then there is no harm if they follow their Truth. Sadly many religions do not allow a soul to do so. I have to say for me that is a great sadness. They believe they are doing the work of the Oneness. They cannot see that to condemn another religion or judge another as they do, they can not see that that is not a Truth to any soul. In a sense those souls are also in their own little thunderstorm. This leads on again to 'Waking up!' We are all being given the opportunities to wake up once and for all. There is no going back to sleep. It is crunch time. That is why, me and many like me, must bring this message through to those that are awake, to give that Love, to wake up those other souls.

We give thanks to the Divine Oneness for allowing this meeting to take place. We ask always that we may remain humble in order to serve and that we may continue to walk in the Light and the Love.

Until we speak again my friends. Carry on laughing!

Adieu, my friend, Adieu.

CHAPTER 36

Throughout the two years it took to put these tapes on to paper, much phenomena occurred. It seemed that not only was I to channel my dearest respected soul White Cloud, but other energies that came from Love that had messages to bring to our world. I chose to leave these tapes aside for now. Maybe another time? another book? who knows?

At the end of the previous chapter, the following comment was made. 'It's nice just to have you for a change White Cloud!'. His reply... 'That is Blossom's sentiment entirely!'

I always specified that if other energies needed to come through, then White Cloud had to be there at the beginning and the end as my gatekeeper. This was always heeded for my protection. At first it was very difficult to work with new energies and sometimes still is.

I found the following words after this comment was made to be the apt ones for the final words from White Cloud for this book.

It was that Blossom was aware earlier that if she chose, others could join us today, but she chose no. I understand this. There are times when one has, as Blossom said, just gone to a new grade, that sometimes you go back and play a piece from the last grade because you can play it well and you know what you are doing. If I may, to clarify to Blossom in this way, there is no cause for alarm, it is merely adjustment that is all. She knows that the trust she has from all of you does not make her any better or worse at what she does. If Blossom chose it could be just me all the time. Another part of Blossom knows that there is more for her to do. This is why the shutters have not been closed. She knows also I would never force her to do anything she did not desire in the name of Love. I would finish by saying that there are plenty of opportunities ahead for myself and Blossom to reach many souls that would not be able initially to understand the wherefores and whereabouts of our other friends. I will always be with her to guide, protect and Love her. I thank her with every part of my being.

Adieu, my friends, Adieu.